PREPARING
FOR
Reentry

PREPARING FOR *Reentry*

WHAT LAWYERS° NEED TO KNOW TO NAVIGATE THE ROAD AHEAD AFTER A CAREER BREAK

M. DIANE VOGT

Defending Liberty
Pursuing Justice

Cover design by ABA Publishing

Printed in the United States of America.

13 12 11 10 09 5 4 3 2 1

Library of Congress Cataloging-in-Publication Data

Vogt, M. Diane, 1952-
  Preparing for reentry : what lawyers need to know to navigate the road ahead after a career break / by M. Diane Vogt.
    p. cm.
  ISBN 978-1-59031-955-0 (hard copy : alk. paper) 1. Law—Vocational guidance—United States.   2. Employment re-entry—United States.   I. Title.

KF298.V64 2009
340.023'73—dc22   2009007844

"Life is either a daring adventure or nothing."

Helen Keller

CONTENTS

ACKNOWLEDGMENTS

Every book is a team effort and this one is no exception. I must thank my wonderful editor, Tim Brandhorst, for contacting me with this project. His vision guided us every step of the way from concept to completion.

My colleague and friend, Lori-Ann Rickard, who supported me through the inevitable research and writing fatigue helped me to focus on the important aspects of a subject we both know way too much about. And to each and every ConnectWell Consulting LLC client and colleague—you make work a joy every day.

All of the amazing lawyers who were willing to discuss these subjects with me over the past twenty-eight years are too numerous to thank here, but you know who you are.

Gratitude goes first, last, and always, to Robert. My partner in every-thing. You're still the one.

INTRODUCTION: THE REAR VIEW MIRROR AND THE ROAD AHEAD

When I begin planning something new or desire to uplevel my game, I eschew unworkable ideas and unproven theories. Instead, I ask an experienced player to tell me what works, show me how I can get it done, and guide me through the quick and easy way. Thousands of lawyers I've worked with do the same. Don't you?

This book contains everything I wish I'd known as my legal career developed over the past twenty-eight years about taking voluntary and involuntary breaks from legal work and returning successfully to a practice even better than the one I left. Looking back, I see now that my career included several time outs, both voluntary and not. My first planned break delayed the outset of my career. I'd already taken three years off between college and law school. After graduation, I negotiated a nine-week delayed start date, planning to study and take the bar, take a vacation, and report for work two weeks afterward. The large general-practice firm in Detroit that had hired me was nonplussed. A new associate had never failed to start along with the rest of the class. The management committee let me know they were somewhat scandalized. I worried that I would never regain their confidence. But I'd worked full-time through law school, and I was simply exhausted. The mere idea of trying to study for the bar, commuting ninety minutes each day to a job I would need to learn from the ground up, and dedicating the number of work hours required was too much for me to contemplate without a break.

When I did join the firm, I felt able to make a full commitment. Indeed, I loved the job and the work. It was eighteen months before I had another day off, and two years before I took another vacation. I loved every minute I spent being a lawyer. The firm supported me, too. I was only the fourth woman they'd ever hired. I became the first woman ever to make equity partner on time. The only other woman partner worked for more than twenty years before she was voted into partnership, and she'd retired long before I was offered a seat at the partnership table. The other two women ahead of me moved on. After four years, I became the most senior woman in the firm.

Many lawyers at this firm took career breaks. I was heavily involved in recruiting, hiring, mentoring, and training lawyers at all levels of practice. We developed and implemented the firm's first maternity leave policy and first family leave policy. We hired lawyers who were embarking on second careers, who had been out of work for various reasons, and who wanted to move to our firm from other firms. Our own staff, associates, and partners took breaks for health reasons, travel, to follow a spouse to another state, rear children, care for family members, and other reasons. Each reentry was handled individually and agreeably.

The next time I took a career break was involuntary. I'd been practicing seven years at the same firm. I'd been teaching trial advocacy at Wayne Law School and simultaneously sitting second chair on a complicated construction case in a sixteen-month jury trial out of town. The class ended in early December (although I taught it five more times over the next few years); the trial ended successfully two weeks before Christmas and three weeks before I was scheduled to make equity partner. I suddenly found myself with a great deal of empty time, which was great for the holiday season, but unnerving when the new year began and I had no work to do. Rebuilding my practice took longer than I expected, partly because I was presented with another involuntary seven-month work gap the following April when I broke my leg. Three years later, the need to care for my dying father who lived in another state took me physically away from the practice for several months. Emotionally, I was away much longer.

After each of these breaks, I returned to the same practice group in the same firm where I'd worked for more than twelve years. Each time, I had to rebuild my practice, but I did so among colleagues who knew me and my work. It wasn't simple, but I felt supported by the firm. Eventually, I left the Detroit firm. Rebuilding my practice yet again was going more slowly than I'd hoped. I decided that rebuilding in a warmer climate made more sense for me. After negotiating the career break, I joined one partner and we built a national boutique litigation practice with offices in Tampa. We quickly ramped up and hired a total of nine lawyers, including a couple of part-timers and a few students, twelve paralegals, and a sizeable support staff.

Three years after we launched our practice, our major client unexpectedly filed for bankruptcy protection. This stopped all work and left us with another involuntary career break. While we'd practiced together, my partner and I had discovered significant differences in our personal styles, desired client base, and preferred working environments. The client's bankruptcy gave me the opportunity for change. I focused on developing better strategies to achieve the quality of life, practice quality, and personal fulfillment issues that had become increasingly important to me. Although I was willing to make these changes inside the firm we had in place, my partner was not.

Thus I began my own firm, structured to suit my developing knowledge of the characteristics of a great, well-balanced law practice. Since 1995, I've owned my own national boutique practice representing Fortune 500 companies, smaller businesses, and individuals in a variety of litigation matters. I've been fortunate to attract some of the best clients of my career and colleagues with whom I enjoy working. My husband and I have become snowbirds, living several months out of the year alternately in Florida and Michigan for more than a decade. We've traveled extensively and made every effort to enjoy our lives as much as possible. Fulfilling a lifelong dream, I've become a published author of both fiction and nonfiction. I've met many of my favorite authors, appeared on television and radio, and spoken at huge conferences of readers. Financially, every move has been significantly and substantially more rewarding than its predecessor. Balancing work and life has not always been easy, but it's been successful for us.

Many lawyers who were managing large and mid-sized law firms asked me how I'd improved my own job satisfaction and how they could do the same. Eventually, with my friend and colleague, Lori-Ann Rickard, We formed PeopleWealth, a partnership legal consulting business focused on law firms. We urged firms to keep good lawyers on board through job satisfaction to stem the alarming rise in lawyer attrition. Several years later, ConnectWell Consulting LLC (http://www.connectwellconsulting. com) expanded our reach to individual lawyers and groups. We assist lawyers who desire to uplevel their practices from good to great; those who want to get well connected to legal industry insiders; and those who want to let the voice of experience guide them to greater skills, better clients, higher profitability, life balance, and improved job satisfaction.

We use experience and expertise to keep good lawyers well connected to extraordinary careers. With thousands of lawyers around the country. In every presentation I've made to large groups of lawyers, I ask how long they've been practicing law. While many are negotiating the first five years of practice, there's always at least one who has practiced for more than forty years. Some have practiced law over fifty or sixty years. Most have taken more than one career break and successfully negotiated reentry themselves.

Drawing from my experiences, from my colleagues around the country, and from current research by several reputable organizations, I've pulled together the best and most useful information, suggestions, tools, tips, and techniques to help you navigate your own successful reentry. These are the things I wish I'd known along the way. I hope you find them helpful as you travel the road ahead. Please write to me and share your successes.

CHAPTER 1

Return of the Champions

Law practices these days are revolving doors for lawyers. Lateral moves by partners are more prevalent than ever before. Famous and infamous lawyers have taken nontraditional, nonlinear paths in droves.

Once you begin talking with lawyers about their careers, you will find a few who have remained in one practice or moved directly from one job to another. But you will also find lawyers who, like the general population, have left a position without having another lined up, or who moved into a completely different field and later returned to law practice or other work. For instance, it's difficult to find a legislator who isn't a lawyer. Lawyers work in accounting firms, consulting firms, banking, brokerage, and countless other fields. Some practiced law initially, some didn't. Family businesses employ lawyers who practiced, then didn't, and now do. In short, despite what you may have heard, not only is reentry conceivable, it's done all the time.

For example, recently, I was asked to present a mentoring workshop with a co-presenter assigned to me by the seminar company. The co-presenter was a lawyer, now working in his fourth law firm as a lawyer and chief recruiting officer. He'd taken three years between law jobs two and three to work in his own consulting firm.

I hired a property lawyer to help me with some boundary issues on an investment lot near my home. He'd been out of law school for seven years. He'd worked in a big Chicago-area law firm for two years, left for quality-of-life reasons to work in his family's golf resort business for four years, and then returned to work as a lawyer in another state. "I like practicing law better now than I ever did before," he said, citing the

1

improved quality of life he experienced in the smaller practice located in a resort town.

A single mother left her job as a junior partner in a large firm for a corporate legal position to have more time with her kids and less business travel. After ten years, she was downsized when the industry went through a rough economic cycle. She spent a few months considering her reentry and started her own very successful boutique health-care practice.

Another single mother left her law firm associate job because while doing "stultifying" bond work, she said, "I was so bored I couldn't stand it." She took a job as a college instructor and began to write romance novels. Now, her two children are grown and she's a best-selling novelist many times over.

On a plane flight to New York City this summer, my seatmate was a lawyer from Chicago. She'd started at a big law firm, decided she didn't like real estate law, left to work in the financial aid department of a small school, and was about to return to her big-firm practice in another department where she thought she'd be better suited to the pace, the clients, and the substantive work.

Seated at a luncheon recently, the daughter of a best-selling novelist told me she was a lawyer on a break. She'd practiced for six years in Washington, D.C., and left her high-powered job to pursue her dream of writing fiction. She did contract work from time to time, but otherwise didn't intend to return to the active practice of law now that she'd sold her first novel. She owned her own home and kept her expenses low to avoid the financial necessity of returning to full-time law practice. She was single and childless, which she was enjoying "for now."

A senior lawyer, single, who enjoys sailing, does legal research and writing for a small firm owned by a long-time friend "whenever my Visa bill gets too high," but otherwise doesn't plan to practice. He defines exactly what work he will do, and when he will do it, and never compromises.

The number of women taking maternity leaves (often more than once) from and returning to large law firms after three to twelve months has been steadily rising since the late 1970s.

A woman lawyer who loved her work, but wanted to try something different, left her large-firm practice after four years to create a consulting firm advising large law firms on techniques to advance women in business. After two years in her consulting business, which she ran from her home office while her son had a full-time nanny, she found she missed law practice. She interviewed with several firms, was hired as an associate, and returned to large-firm practice, although she "took a financial hit because I had to go back four class levels instead of two for the years I'd spent in another industry. That's the bad news. The good news is that it didn't take me long to catch up."

A husband and wife, both lawyers, decided to enjoy a bit of freedom before starting a family. He left his job at a brokerage house; she quit her job as an associate at a large firm. They rustled up some contract legal work they could do remotely from time to time, rented out their home, put their possessions in storage, and took off for a year to travel the U.S. When they came back, both returned to practice and continue to practice today. She continues to do contract legal work from home while she cares for their two young children. He owns his own practice.

Another couple, she a lawyer and he a software designer, took off a year to live in the Dominican Republic. Both returned to the U.S. and to work and have moved into new jobs since their initial reentry positions.

Confirming these anecdotal reports, Harvard Business School published *Off-Ramps and On-Ramps* by Sylvia Ann Hewlett in 2007. The book is filled with statistics and other data supporting the business case for a nonlinear career path. Hewlett reports that two-thirds of women take short career breaks or reduced workloads during some portion of their careers.

All of these lawyers and thousands more have done exactly what you're considering now. They took a break from the practice of law and then successfully reentered the workforce. What they've done, you can do, too.

PowerPlay: Realize that taking a career break isn't the end of your legal career. Talk to other lawyers and you'll find many who've done exactly what you're seeking to do now.

PlugIn: Get clear on your motivation. Why haven't you returned to work? Why do you want to do it now?

Recommended Resources: *The Comeback: Seven Stories of Women Who Went from Career to Family and Back Again*, by Emma Gilbey Keller, 2008 (Bloomsbury USA, 2008); *Off-Ramps and On-Ramps: Keeping Talented Women on the Road to Success*, by Sylvia Ann Hewlett (Harvard Business School Press, 2007).

Best Fresh Tip: Do you have grit? People with grit are more likely to achieve, maybe because their passion and commitment help them endure through setbacks. Develop grit by making a commitment and sticking with it.

CHAPTER 2

Reenter Your Ideal Platinum Practice™

Preparing to reenter the workforce after a break in service is the next phase of a long, well-balanced life. Meaningful work is as essential to a life worth living as self care and family care. The issue for lawyers considering reentry is: what is strategically next in my ideal career?

As a practicing lawyer in a variety of settings for more than twenty-eight years, I've spent a great deal of time learning, speaking, consulting, and teaching about successful law practices and lawyer job satisfaction. Although strategies for creating the perfect law practice have evolved significantly, one traditional truth is undeniable: responsibility for creating a satisfying career lies solidly with the individual lawyer. While this is a truth many lawyers resist, we should embrace the responsibility because we can then create the careers we desire rather than being forced into square holes for which we are often ill-suited round pegs. Speaking from experience, I can say unequivocally that well-satisfied lawyers are those who feel they have control over their lives and their careers. This is partially due to the lawyer personality (more on this later), but also reflects the high-pressure lives we all live in the twenty-first century's global technology economy.

While researching a co-authored book on this subject, I interviewed lawyers in all types of practices. They were asked to rate their overall job satisfaction, and then to indicate, on a scale of one to ten, their levels of satisfaction in several aspects of practice. Lawyers who rated themselves as "very well satisfied" also rated their practices at the top end of the scale on "flexibility" and "control." They achieved job satisfaction through active management of their careers, including creating a job where they had maximum flexibility and control over their practices. This was true whether they worked in private practice, corporate law departments, consulting, government, or the non-profit sector. It was also true of males and females in all environments. (More on this later, too.)

When the individual lawyer sets the tone for his or her practice, taking control and creating a practice that suits his or her needs at every stage of practice and at every stage of life, then job satisfaction is possible. In other words, well-satisfied lawyers make career satisfaction their number one goal when focusing on career issues, and life satisfaction their number one goal overall.

In the context of lawyers seeking to reenter the workforce after a break in employment for whatever reason, research and experience proves that the individual lawyer will be most satisfied with the reentry when she or he takes the time to figure out what type of work will best suit her or his needs and how to create that job at this juncture.

What the reentering lawyer should seek is what I've come to call a Platinum Practice™: a practice that is the best possible version of your ideal practice at this stage in your life and career. This is a strategic decision, not a linear path. In other words, what's next in your career is totally up to you. There is no norm you must achieve.

In this slim volume, using some humor, a few statistics, significant experiences, and unique expertise, we'll take a brief tour of preparing for reentry to your Platinum Practice™. Don't expect doom and gloom here; there's plenty of that in both the lawyer personality and the world as it is. Instead, we're seeking to take it easy. When I was a new lawyer, I worked with a talented mentor who told me repeatedly: "Diane, there are two ways to do everything, the easy way and the hard way." He was right. Throughout my career, I've learned the hard way that the easy way is always best. Thus, my definition of Platinum Practice™ includes a relaxed, low-stress atmosphere.

Beyond the truth that doing things the easy way suits my personality (and yours, I'm betting), science proves that we learn better and remember what we've learned longer when we're having an emotional, multisensory experience. Of course, we can do this the easy way or the hard way. We could scare ourselves into returning to work at jobs we hate in order to justify our sacrifices, ignore our health, shortchange our families, and abandon our communities. Fear and negative experiences embed themselves in our memories easily and firmly. I've had business partners and clients who use fear to motivate themselves and others. They are sometimes at the top of the wealth and status pyramid. They're also divorced (multiple times), lonely, unhappy, socially dysfunctional, and quite often reviled. No thank you. Not for me.

Joy, laughter, and positive experiences also embed themselves in our memories, but they take a little more effort. This is one reason it's harder to remember jokes than horror stories. Yet, lawyers who make the effort to create a career they enjoy are happy, have successful family lives, plenty of money, good clients, and good relationships with colleagues. Personally, I've decided that extra effort is worth it. Years ago, I chose this path. I invite you to join me as you prepare for reentry into the next phase of your lifelong relationship with work, your version of Platinum Practice™. This book is short and you'll enjoy the time we spend together. If you decide to take the fear road after trying the joy road, that's okay, too. But try the easy way. Give it a chance. It could work for you the way it's worked for thousands of others in all walks of life. Really, what have you got to lose?

PowerPlay: Ask better questions as you plan your reentry strategy. In a world where anything can be done, what's worth doing? What is strategically (not just logically) next? Who can help you? What is the easiest way to get to the next destination?

PlugIn: Join the Platinum Practice™ community at http://www.connectwellconsulting.com for innovative strategic solutions, information, and tips that work.

Recommended Resource: *Keeping Good Lawyers: Best Practices to Create Career Satisfaction,* by M. Diane Vogt and Lori-Ann Rickard (Law Practice Management Section, American Bar Association, 2000).

Best Fresh Tip: Take the joy road, the easy way, to creating your Platinum Practice™.

CHAPTER 3

Making the Most of the Lawyer Personality

What is the lawyer personality? Intuitively, lawyers recognize many of the lawyer personality's attributes. Understanding and using the most common aspects of the lawyer personality is a powerful strategy when contemplating and creating your new Platinum Practice™.

How many times have you heard that managing lawyers is like herding cats? Psychologists have studied lawyers extensively and confirmed that lawyers do resemble cats in many personality aspects. The Caliper Personality Profile has been applied to thousands of lawyers. Oversimplifying, lawyers consistently score in the 90th percentile on "skepticism," a characteristic that is essential to our work. We tend to be skeptical, cynical, judgmental, questioning, argumentative, and self-protective. This skepticism characteristic serves us well when dealing with our adversaries, but doesn't serve us as well in cooperative environments or when designing our lives and careers. Understanding skepticism in ourselves and in the lawyers with whom we work helps us to deal effectively with the conflict inherent in law practice and to choose the level of conflict with which we're comfortable when we choose our next work environment.

Lawyers score almost as high in measures of "autonomy," meaning we resist being managed, bristle at being told what to do, and revel in our independence. Sounds like cats, doesn't it? Again, this trait is extremely useful in our lawyer as advocate roles, but not as helpful to our relationships and life goals. Our autonomy strength can lead lawyers into dysfunctional independence and unnecessarily overburden both personal and professional resources. We make the mistake of doing too much ourselves because we believe that we can do the job better than anyone else. Misunderstood and unchecked, overactive autonomy leads to lawyer burnout. Many lawyers on a break left due to burnout and now seek reentry into a less stressful environment. Recognizing that lawyers tend to lead themselves in this direction expands our options because once acknowledged and understood, we have the opportunity to keep autonomy in check.

Speaking of relationships, on the Caliper Profile, lawyers tend to score very low in measures of "resilience" or "ego strength," meaning we tend to be defensive and hypersensitive to criticism while we resist feedback. If you've ever received or delivered a performance review, you probably recognize these characteristics from your own feelings or the reactions from others. This trait can be less than helpful when job hunting, for example, because we feel the inevitable rejections too keenly.

Lawyers also score low on "sociability," which reflects that we prefer enjoying our existing relationships rather than establishing new ones. We like spending time with information more than people, and we are more comfortable emphasizing the intellect over emotions. It is important to realize that law practice is a relationship business. Clients hire the lawyer, not the firm, and clients hire lawyers they know and trust. Anyone who hires you is, by definition, your client. This includes, for example, lawyers senior to you and referring relationships such as friends, colleagues, and other professionals or acquaintances. To build a successful law practice of any kind, lawyers must develop a wide circle of relationships. This means leaving our comfort zones, which many people are reluctant to do and lawyers often loathe.

According to Dr. Daniel Goleman, author of the 1995 best-selling book *Emotional Intelligence*, which is a little too touchy-feely for many skeptical lawyers, those who regularly and consistently try to understand themselves, seek feedback, and gain insight into their own inner emotional responses are significantly more successful in life. While lawyers may resist emotional intelligence concepts, we are more effective when we understand and employ them.

There is one more piece of the lawyer personality puzzle relevant to potential reentry: the character trait scientists call "optimism bias." On November 9, 2007, *The Wall Street Journal* reported findings published by Duke University in the *Journal of Financial Economics*, quoting Duke Finance Scholar David T. Robinson, "A little bit of optimism is associated with a lot of positive economic choices." Another pair of researchers at New York University studied neural activity using fMRI technology to conclude, "[O]ur brains imagine positive future events about our own well-being more intensely and vividly than negative possibilities." Indeed, the article's author, Robert Lee Hotz, pointed out, "The influence of optimism on human behavior is so pervasive that it must have survival value, researchers speculate, and may give us the ability to act in the face of uncertain odds."

Here is the relevant piece for our purposes: The researchers' conclusion was that optimists do better in life than pessimists—except for lawyers. Hotz reported, "Surveying law students at the University of Virginia [Dr. Martin Seligman, University of Pennsylvania] found that pessimists got better grades, were more likely to make law review and, upon graduation, received better job offers. There was no scientific reason. 'In law,' he said, 'pessimism is considered prudence.'"

Although this description of the lawyer personality is a very brief and oversimplified description of more complicated research and testing instruments, doesn't it sound at least a bit like you and other lawyers you know?

Now that you're aware that these characteristics are inherent in the lawyer personality, you're equipped to deal more effectively with them as you consider reentry into your Platinum Practice™. Use this information in two ways: to evaluate your own behavior and reactions, and to evaluate the behavior and reactions of other lawyers you approach or with whom you interact. As you go through the rest of this book, use your strong lawyer personality traits to evaluate the information you receive. But also recognize that those traits can hold you back and prevent you from creating a satisfying career if you allow them to push your buttons without restraint. Once you become aware of your habitual reactions and learn to rely upon the trustworthy ones, you will have a significant advantage when preparing to reenter the working world. Also use your knowledge of the lawyer personality to evaluate the feedback you get from others. For example, when discussing your initial plans to reenter the workforce with lawyer colleagues, realize they are prone to be skeptical and to advise you based upon their own strong autonomy values. While such advice may be spot on, it may be a bit too jaded. Remember that your ultimate reentry goal is to create your ideal Platinum Practice™, which will suit your life. As such, your opinion is paramount.

PowerPlay: Begin to consider developing your lifelong Platinum Practice™ as you contemplate reentry, using more optimism and less pessimism.

PlugIn: Knowing lawyers are skeptical by nature suggests you may be looking for proof of this information right now. For a revealing explanation of common traits of the lawyer personality, see "Herding Cats: The Lawyer Personality Revealed," an article by Larry R. Richard (Hildebrandt International Publications/Press Room, 2009), at http://hildebrandt.com/Documents.aspx?Doc_ID=2430.

Recommended Resource: For further insight into the relationship of psychology and the practice of law, read *Authentic Happiness*, by Martin E. P. Seligman (Free Press, 2004).

Best Fresh Tip: Recognize the common aspects of the lawyer personality and use them effectively when creating your Platinum Practice™.

CHAPTER 4

Getting Your Head in the Game: Part One

There are two types of relevant information that fall under the broad rubric of the head games we're talking about here: physical brain function and psychology. Brain sciences are continually evolving. It seems researchers learn more every day, and often the new material conflicts with prior knowledge or may be totally contradictory. Lawyers are tempted to ignore the soft sciences because we feel uncomfortable with nonobjective material, and await further scientific discovery of physiology. Doing so is nothing more than a procrastination technique holding you back from a successful Platinum Practice™. Both physiological brain functions and the psychology of personal change occur whether we understand them or not.

As lawyers, we learn through acquisition of at least minimal intellectual comprehension. We don't need to be rocket scientists to write a will for an astronaut, but we do need to know that the astronaut is involved with spaceships and gravity in a high-risk activity, suggesting that preflight estate planning would be prudent. Similarly, when engineering your own reentry after a career break, it helps to know that when humans follow a dream or change a habit, we pass through five stages social scientists call precontemplation (we don't know we want or need to change), contemplation (we think we'll change "someday"), preparation (we'll change "soon"), action (we start now), and maintenance (achieve the goal and stay there).

Consider your own status at the moment. What stage of reentering the workforce are you in? It's unlikely you are at the precontemplation stage because you're reading this book. If you didn't know you wanted or needed to change, you wouldn't be reading. It is most likely that you are in the contemplation or preparation phase of the process. From here, you may remain in either of these phases indefinitely or move to action. Whether you take consistent action and stick with your plan until you achieve the maintenance phase is also up to you.

On the physiology side, the brain's function has been described most usefully for purposes of illustrating this point in three parts: the reptilian brain, which controls basic physiology such as your heartbeat without your conscious intervention; the emotional brain, where feelings reside that bring pleasure and pain as well as the urges to fight or flight; and the thinking brain, where reason resides and where lawyers generate most of their conscious life experiences, somewhat unaware that their emotional brains are also contributing to the mix. The lawyer personality, as well as our trained objectivity and detachment, lures us toward the thinking brain. But the emotional brain, like the reptilian brain, is doing its thing, whether we notice it or not.

Anyone who has ever failed to complete or maintain a physical fitness program, for example, has experienced the conflict between the thinking brain and the emotional brain. Your thinking brain decided to work out, you made a plan and maybe started the program, but at some point you quit. Your thinking brain rationalized that you lacked the time, the money, the energy or the desire to achieve your goals and maintain your fitness plan. Yet, the real reason you quit that program and any others you may have failed to follow through with is that your emotional brain didn't cooperate with your plan. You just didn't feel like continuing. The plan was too hard, too scary, or wasn't fun; or the pain of continuing was greater than the anticipated pain of quitting. When an obstacle arose, the effort/reward connection wasn't strong enough to keep you emotionally engaged. You quit because quitting felt better than continuing.

To achieve a successful reentry, you will need a better strategy. Whether you are in the contemplation, preparation, action, or maintenance phases of reentry, make a plan with your thinking brain but get your emotional brain on board. Without an emotional connection, reentry is destined to fail. When both thinking and emotions work together, a successful outcome is assured.

Nothing is ever accomplished without enthusiasm and desire. Until you create a strategic plan that you can believe in, are emotionally identified with, and are enthusiastic about, your reentry has little chance to happen at all, let alone succeed. To break the bonds of inertia, choose emotionally engaging and satisfying desires.

Once you have harnessed your thinking and emotional brains and traveled through the first three stages of preparation, you will be energized to set goals and take action. Go for easy, fun, exciting, new, and worthwhile.

Let's take a closer look at worthwhile goals for a moment. Research suggests that humans are hardwired to avoid pain and seek pleasure. Many humans will work harder to avoid pain than to seek pleasure, whether they realize they're doing so or not. Goals can be framed as either pain avoidance or pleasure seeking. Be strategic in designing your goals. Work with framing a goal in several ways to see how it feels to you, whether you can get excited about it or not. The more excited you are, the more likely you are to follow through, and the more likely the goal is to carry you over the long road from here to there.

How can you tell the difference between a fear-avoidance goal and a pleasure-seeking goal? Does it matter? Can a goal be worthwhile either way? Consider again a hypothetical physical fitness plan. After a health scare, such as a heart attack or cancer, people are very likely to get energized about physical fitness, to take action, and to maintain their new healthy habits. This is blatant fear-avoidance motivation: people discover they don't want to die just yet and must take better care of themselves to live. A powerful motivator for a worthwhile goal, don't you think? Remember I told you that fear motivation works, especially for lawyers.

But what about the woman who wants to be thin for her wedding or the fellow who wants to look good for his class reunion? Are those fear-avoidance goals or pleasure-seeking goals? I'd say they're fear-avoidance goals because both have as their underlying element the fear that others won't approve or will judge them harshly unless they become something they aren't right now. The goals are nevertheless worthwhile and likely to be accomplished, at least temporarily, if the fear is strong enough.

The problem with fear-avoidance goals is that they often come with a heavy stress price tag. Achieving fear-avoidance goals doesn't make us feel better. We continue to fear the thing we're keeping at bay by achieving the goal temporarily. Fear-avoidance goals are Faustian bargains. We are selling our souls to the devil for a relatively cheap price, giving our lives away for too little reward. Fear-avoidance goals cause resentment, anger, and anxiety, and can lead to debilitating depression or substance abuse. Fear does motivate us. But I don't recommend it as a method for deliberately creating a long, healthy, satisfying life and career. Olympic athletes don't win gold medals by fearing what will happen if they lose.

Pleasure-seeking goals are more fun, exciting, and fruitful. When we pursue them, the action of striving itself is rewarding. They make us happy, and when we're happy everyone wins. We'll talk more about happiness later, but for now, suffice it to say that research shows happy people live longer, have better relationships, are healthier, and more successful, too. This is a radical idea for lawyers because lawyers are heavily invested in helping others through personal sacrifice, not through pursuing happiness. Lawyers work long, hard hours because they believe their clients depend on them, and they can't let the clients down—even if serving the client means going without sleep, eating poorly, and missing important family gatherings. Lawyers on a career break who are in the contemplation, preparation, and half-hearted-action stages are often ambivalent about returning to work because they don't want to rejoin the self-sacrifice cycle, no matter how worthy potential client causes might be.

I submit to you that no worthy human achievement has ever occurred without significant enthusiasm for a pleasure-seeking goal. The best lawyers work long hours because they take pride in and feel good about helping others. They like what the money they honestly earn can do for their own families. These lawyers make time for a balanced life because a balanced life makes them and their loved ones feel good, and, well, happy. Everybody wins.

PowerPlay: Determine which phase of the reentry process you're resting in now and whether you're ready to move to the next phase. If you're not ready now, when will you be ready?

PlugIn: Give yourself some deadlines for moving through each of the phases of reentry. The length of time you spend in each phase is less important than moving forward. Will you remain where you are for another hour? Another year? Creating a deadline will keep the goal on your mental radar and help you make progress.

Recommended Resource: *Happiness: Unlocking the Mysteries of Psychological Wealth,* by Ed Diener and Robert Biswas-Diener (Wiley-Blackwell, 2008).

Best Fresh Tip: Consider framing your goals as pleasure seeking rather than pain avoidance, to increase desire and enthusiasm and prepare for achievement. How does the more positive frame make you feel? Can your emotional brain get behind the pleasure-seeking process? Can your thinking brain get out of the way?

CHAPTER 5

Getting Your Head in the Game: Part Two

Brain science now confirms that habits and behaviors are embedded in the brain through pathways created when we experience life. The more we experience something with all of our senses, the stronger the pathway we create in our brain.

We don't think a pathway to learning multiplication tables, we experience practicing the multiplication tables through flash cards or computer games and homework. We don't think ourselves into bike riding, we experience learning to balance on our first bike and learning to control it. Once we develop the muscle memory and the brain pathways needed to recite the multiplication tables or ride a bike, we can ignore multiplication or bike riding for years and pick them up again easily. The pathway might be a little rusty, but it's still there.

Think about a song you learned in high school when you knew the lyrics by heart. Maybe the song that was playing when you received your first meaningful kiss or when your team won the state championship. If the song plays on the radio tomorrow, you'll remember the lyrics and sing along as if you'd learned them yesterday instead of decades ago. Since high school, you've learned hundreds of song lyrics or maybe thousands. But the old lyrics are still there, embedded in your brain, along with all the newer lyrics you learned afterward, and with room for all of the new lyrics you'll learn before you die.

This is so of all habits and routines, skills and activities. Once again, understanding this truth is a source of power for your reentry. Reentry is a set of new skills you'll need to learn. New habits and routines will need to be acquired. Your life has changed since you took a break from practicing law. Law practice has changed, too. There will be a different workplace, with new colleagues and clients. These changes will present challenges and opportunities, but your learning curve will not be as steep as the learning slope you climbed fresh out of law school. The skills you developed when you were practicing are still there, even if you haven't accessed them in a while. You can build on those. If you apply a few simple techniques, rebuilding won't be too difficult.

One such technique is precise visualization. Medal-winning athletes have known for decades that sports success is a mental game. The right mental approach is at least as important to championship play in any arena as physical talent and training. An amazing study done with the 1976 Olympic ski team established that precise-visualization training can actually be more effective and less stressful than physical training. As a result, precise-visualization techniques have become a standard training tool for athletes.

Athletes and their trainers know that precise visualization reduces stress and anxiety, enhances motivation, heightens planning, and facilitates peak performance. Precise visualization can do the same for you at all stages of your reentry process. Effective precise visualization contains four elements: correct, precise, vivid, and distributed. What you visualize must be correctly performed. Only perfect practice makes perfect performance. You must first know what perfect performance is before you can correctly attempt it, but you should not under any circumstances visualize failure. Visualizing the perfect failure leads to that precise failure, too. Precisely visualize the activities and behaviors you need to perform to move you to the next level of the process. For example, if you are ready to move from preparation into action, visualize calling a specific hiring person at your specific ideal potential employer to schedule an interview. See yourself engaging in the conversation, explaining why you want to meet, dealing with any likely objections, and persisting in the face of rejection until he or she is persuaded to meet with you. See yourself setting up the time and place for the meeting and then concluding the call. Vividly imagine the scene as if you were really living it. Think it, feel it, act it. Put yourself in the visualization and experience everything that happens. If you feel anxious or uncomfortable during the exercise, figure out why and fix it. Don't keep visualizing something that doesn't make you feel energized, enthused, and ready to move ahead.

Distribute your visualizations in short bursts over a long period of time for the greatest impact. Like learning to play a musical instrument, you must train your muscles and your emotions as well as your mind. Creating the appropriate muscle memory and new brain pathways for your new behavior doesn't happen in one session, no matter how intense that session is.

Depending on your current stage of psychological change, you may find this chapter mildly interesting, or amusing, or even be tempted to dismiss visualization and brain pathways because your lawyer's personality is skeptical. Yet, these are powerful truths, well established in the scientific and athletic worlds. I can tell you from experience they actually work. At minimum, research the concepts for yourself before you dismiss them.

At the contemplation stage, there's very little risk to giving precise visualization a try. A stay-at-home mom, for example, might visualize leaving her son with a loving, trusted caregiver. She might watch the child enjoy his day with delighted amusement, a joy she can virtually share if she feels strongly satisfied that her son is thriving while Mommy is away. Over time, Mommy will feel less separation anxiety about returning to work.

In the preparation stage, you're ready to create and precisely visualize your perfect reentry position until you're inspired to move into the action phase. Understanding the importance of creating and using your brain's pathways and practicing visualization can reduce your reentry anxiety significantly as well as move you more quickly to your goals. Beyond that, it's fun.

PowerPlay: Get your head in the game by using your thinking brain to craft an optimistic plan exciting to your emotional brain. Use precise visualization to experience and refine the plan as well as reduce any potential stress associated with implementing the plan.

PlugIn: Avoid commiserating with or wallowing in any form of negativity while you're planning and seeking reentry, because precise visualization works to create negative as well as positive results. Keep a positive mental attitude and remember Justices O'Connor and Ginsberg when your lawyer's pessimism threatens.

Recommended Resources: *Psychological Foundations of Success: A Harvard-Trained Scientist Separates the Science of Success from Self-Help Snake Oil,* by Stephen Kraus (Next Level Science, 2003).

Best Fresh Tip: Get reconnected to your local bar associations. Attend meetings and mingle with other lawyers. Ask lawyers if they've ever taken a break from the practice of law and, if so, how they managed reentry. The number of success stories you hear will boost your visualization and spirits.

CHAPTER 6

Supreme Role Models

Despite gender wage gaps, attrition statistics, workplace inequities, and limited advancement potential, there has never been a better time to be a woman lawyer in America. If you've taken a break from the practice of law and are thinking about getting back into the game, take heart. No matter what your situation, your reentry is not only possible, it can be an amazing process if you design it to be.

Lest you're tempted to think otherwise, consider that this book could have only four words on every page: Justice Sandra Day O'Connor. She seems like an amazing icon now (and she is), but back in 1952 when she graduated from law school, her future had significantly less potential than her male classmates'. A wife and mother of three sons, she combined a career with her personal life long before such a course was commonly feasible. We all know how her story turned out: she became the first woman on the U.S. Supreme Court. Her friend, William Rehnquist, was valedictorian of their Stanford Law School class and made it to the court first. Although Justice O'Connor's professional path was far more circuitous and less traditional than Rehnquist's, she reached the same destination. He arrived before her, but she outlasted him. She served from 1981 to 2006, while Justice Rehnquist's term was 1971–2005. These days, applying the clarity of hindsight, some scholars even claim that the Rehnquist court was instead the O'Connor court.

What you may not know is that Justice O'Connor took several lengthy breaks from the practice of law. She also worked part-time for many years. When she finally managed to get a job out of law school as a deputy county attorney in San Mateo, her husband was drafted and sent to

Germany. She was out of the U.S. workforce for three years. Then, she started a private practice where she worked part-time. Later, she left her private practice for four years to raise her two children, and had a third child. After this four-year break, during which time she volunteered in various capacities, O'Connor returned to work again, this time in the Arizona Attorney General's office. A while later, she again cut back from full-time to part-time work, which she continued for several years. Then she took a detour. She was appointed to fill a vacant senate seat and reelected twice.

She didn't become a judge until she was elected in 1975. In 1979, she was appointed to the Arizona Court of Appeals. From there, Justice O'Connor was nominated and confirmed to the U.S. Supreme Court in 1981 and served until she retired in 2006. Yes, Justice O'Connor was a trailblazer, a determined woman at a unique time in history. We see that now, but there can be no doubt that she and her family didn't expect her amazing future back when she was seeking to return to work.

Or consider Ruth Bader Ginsberg, another trailblazer with an astonishing career as a lawyer, a wife, and mother of two before being appointed to the Federal bench in 1980 and then the U.S. Supreme Court in 1993. She married in 1954, enrolled at Harvard Law School that same year, and delivered her first child in 1955. Like Justice O'Connor, Justice Ginsberg followed her husband to another city where she enrolled at Columbia Law School to complete her degree. She graduated with an LLB, tied for first in her class. She had a long and varied career, including work as a judicial clerk, as a law school professor, and at the ACLU before becoming the second woman appointed to the U.S. Supreme Court.

Of course, if we wanted to do things the hard way, we could lament the lack of progress women lawyers have made in the past thirty years. There is plenty of evidence to justify a pessimistic outlook. But is that helpful? Does wallowing in the negative statistics make you want to jump up and go back to work? I thought not. Instead, let's try the easy way, shall we?

The message for the rest of us is that if these women could do everything they did, surely women can manage to reenter the workforce after taking a break. Successful reentry examples abound in your local women's bar association. Like Justices O'Connor and Ginsberg, the facts are there, but we're simply not aware of them. After all, women are only going back to work, not trying to become a U.S. Supreme Court justice. Then again, Sandra Day O'Connor and Ruth Bader Ginsberg didn't have their sights set on the Supreme Court, either, so who knows?

PowerPlay: Get inspired. Find extraordinary women lawyers to consider as professional role models, whether you meet them or not. Most have had similar work experiences and have spent time out of the active workforce.

PlugIn: Find a local woman lawyer who has achieved the reentry you hope to accomplish. Schedule a meeting with her and ask her how she managed to do what you seek to do. If you can't find one, contact me, and I'll help you look. Contact me at diane@ connectwellconsulting.com.

Recommended Resource: For more on Justice O'Connor's life and personal struggles with finding work after law school, juggling marriage, three sons, a career in law and politics, and surviving breast cancer, as well as her accomplishments on the Supreme Court, read *Sandra Day O'Connor: Justice in the Balance,* by Ann Carey McFeatters (University of New Mexico Press, 2006).

Best Fresh Tip: Allow inspiration to lead you forward toward your own goals, whether your goals are the same as the achievements of others or not.

CHAPTER 7

The Road Best Traveled

I just returned from lunch with another lawyer who is preparing to transition his practice. In his case, after fifteen years with a large national firm and in the wake of a recent divorce, he plans to change his job, too. His idea is to move from a large firm defense litigation practice to his own shop specializing in plaintiffs' class actions, an area in which he has developed expertise. He's doing several things right to prepare for his transition. First, he's following his heart: he wants to do work that he finds more professionally, personally, and financially rewarding. Second, he's giving himself enough time to make the change: he's not planning to leave his current job for another six months. Third, he's financially prepared to support himself for at least two years as he builds his new practice. All of these strategies will reduce the stress associated with such a change. So far, so good.

There is one gaping hole in his plans, though. He has no idea how or where he will find the new clients he must have to make his dream a reality, which is why he was lunching with me. These new clients, he believes, are the only missing pieces in his plan. But they're a heck of a big piece. He has never generated any clients on his own. For fifteen years, he has serviced the institutional clients of his big firm. He has no real clue how to build the law practice he desires, or even where to begin. Whether he realizes it or not, he's preparing for reentry. Which brings us to the fourth thing he's doing right: asking the right person for the right help, a step many lawyers are reluctant to take.

As we discussed earlier, lawyers are generally independent, self-reliant, self-protective, and more skeptical than 90 percent of the population. These personality traits both support and hinder lawyers in times of change, such as when preparing for reentry. Reentry is that point where a lawyer changes her career, embarking on a totally new path. Whether the new path comes after an extended break in gainful employment or changing from one job to another, it is helpful to realize that one's professional life proceeds along a continuum of work. This is a one-way street that leads only to success. There is no failure and no turning back. Time marches forward; things change whether we like it or not. The question is, where will your work life be when you're 40, 50, 60, 70, 80, and beyond? Life, including work life, is a mental game. After developing basic skills and perfecting those skills to a master level, returning to work after a break is nothing more than creating and executing a great plan. Lawyers are very good at creating and executing great plans. Lawyers like you can do anything and have done everything. If you're worried about the reentry, that, too, is normal.

No doubt you've heard that lawyers are leaving the practice of law in droves. Since at least the mid-1990s, the documented attrition statistics at large law firms where the majority of lawyers are employed have been alarmingly high. In the decade since the first significant studies of this phenomenon were published, attrition statistics have climbed even higher despite efforts to curb them. Thus, if you are one of the thousands of lawyers who've left law practice in the past fifteen years, the good news is that your detour is far from unique. You may feel like a unicorn, but you more closely resemble a thoroughbred: not too unusual, highly specialized, and extremely desirable, even if you still have to find the right racetrack to suit your personal circumstances.

Nor is the situation different in the general workforce population. People leave jobs and other people find new ones every day in all fields, including medicine, law, teaching, business, banking, technology, and countless others. Perhaps you've read data suggesting that women have a tough time successfully returning to work after taking a break to start families or care for parents. While those statistics can be true, they are just as often false. Studies show at least 42 percent of working women take at least one detour during the course of their careers—often more than one. Indeed, a winding course is so normal to modern career development that you *should* contemplate a winding long-term career that complements a successful life.

Two fairly recent societal norms have combined to make your reentry course unremarkable, meaning nothing to worry about. First, the number of women practicing law has skyrocketed since 1980. Women now enter the legal workforce in numbers greater than men. When those women travel the typical nonlinear career paths of women in general, larger numbers of lawyers end up taking a break from their careers rather than following the typical linear career path marched by male lawyers in earlier generations. The new normal has been established, quietly and without fanfare: lawyers don't work from law school to the grave without a break in service anymore, just as lawyers don't remain with the same practice for an entire career.

The second societal issue is our desire, as humans, for work/life balance and the particular emphasis on balance by the well-publicized X and Y generations. In short, younger lawyers are not willing to sacrifice themselves for years in thrall of a payoff decades down the expressway, as the greatest generation did. Baby boomers made practice-hopping normal in their quest for career appreciation, respect, and advancement. Today's generation X and Y lawyers seek personal satisfaction, flexibility, growth, and fun, and they're willing to change jobs until they find it.

Thus, those statistics showing women returning to work after a break for childrearing in lower numbers and taking jobs at lower income levels include women who don't want to get back into the rat race at the same or faster speeds. The statistical wage gap, in fact, begins to emerge only after three years of practice. Women and men are hired at identical salary levels and advance at comparable levels (some women actually make more money than their male peers). A wage gap opens as careers develop and women make work/life balance choices more frequently than men, but men are catching up with women's desire for a balanced life.

Along with several other challenges faced by the legal market, these two changes have created a nearly revolving door of talented lawyers in today's law practices. Current estimates are that at least 20 percent of new hires leave their big firm law jobs each year. More than 80 percent of new hires leave within the first five years of practice. *This is almost twice as much turnover as the alarmingly high rates that appeared ten years ago.* Numbers of lateral lawyer departures and partners hired have also increased. Some job hop from one position to another. But a significant percentage of lawyers, male and female, take breaks from law practice altogether for a variety of reasons.

The stereotypical mommy track is a choice many lawyers make, but often the mommy track is the default choice resulting from poor job satisfaction. When faced with the demands of family versus those of a less-than-enjoyable job, lawyers find it easy to decide to take a break to focus on family. After a break, many lawyers never go back into the practice of law, but many do return, often to practices they enjoy more than ever. Some return to the practices they left behind. More often, lawyers seek new opportunities when they are ready to return to work because they see no reason to return to an unsatisfactory work environment.

If life is a highway and work life a significant portion of the road with all roads leading ultimately to the end of the line, there are nevertheless many routes from here to there and many stretches suitable for varied travel speeds. We're all going to get there. The question is how and when and what we experience on the journey. How do rejoiners do it? That is, what is the well-crafted plan and how do you execute it?

PowerPlay: Recognize and acknowledge your goal as an achievable activity. Work is an essential element of human happiness and a strong element of life balance. Balance is something you do, not something you have; constant effort is required to obtain and maintain balance.

PlugIn: Create a great plan with a strategic execution timeline. Reentry, defined as any major transition from one type of employment or unemployment to reemployment, is inevitable and inevitably successful.

Recommended Resource: From *Back on the Career Track,* by Carol Fishman Cohen and Vivian Steir Rabin (Business Plus, 2007), page 206:"We estimate that there are over 2.1 million former career women currently at home who are interested in relaunching. . . . [This] indicates to potential relaunchers on a career break that they are far from alone, and it tells employers that this cohort of women is a force to be reckoned with from a hiring perspective." (Also at http://backonthecareertrack.com/.)

Best Fresh Tip: Unsure of what new jobs to consider? Check out the Caliper Profile (http://caliperonline.com/), a personality profiling method used to profile more than 1,000 lawyers. Harold Weinstein, chief operating officer of Caliper Corporation, noted that "People who are working in roles that are consistent with their personality, values and interpersonal characteristics generally outperform those who are less well matched—by a ratio of two-to-one."

CHAPTER 8

Timing the Trip

You've heard the question before. When is the best time to plant an oak tree? Answer: Twenty years ago. Next question: When is the second best time to plant an oak tree? Answer: Now.

The point is that the best time to plan a reentry to law practice is before you take your break. If you're reading this book because you're thinking about taking a break and making such a plan to reenter, good for you. You'll have many more options for reentry if you're going about the process in advance. The easiest place to reenter is the practice you left, assuming you left on good terms and made preparations to return after your absence. This is often done with short maternity or paternity leaves, for example. Most law practices have such leave policies in place and they are used effectively.

Be aware that policies for working part-time in large law practices are not as effectively utilized. Whether part-time work arrangements will suit your situation and, if so, whether a particular firm actually encourages the use of such policies are questions you'll need to ask before you accept the job. It is unusual for large firms to hire a lawyer specifically to work part-time. Smaller firms or temporary agencies are more likely employers for part-time lawyers.

Perhaps you plan a break to travel the African continent, or climb a mountain, or work on a political campaign, or start a business, or write fiction and nonfiction. If you know that you will return within a set period of time, you can often negotiate your long-term leave and return in advance.

Note that planning to reenter the same practice you left doesn't mean taking up where you left off. Practice policies vary widely, and there is usually room for individual negotiation. Some practices will allow you to rejoin at the same level you left. Some advance you along with the rest of your class during your absence. Others penalize you for the time off because they feel that you have not advanced at the same rate as the other members of your class during your absence, which may be true. What actually happens in each individual case is a matter of policy and negotiation.

Also note that the assumptions upon which any underlying policy is based may not apply to your particular situation. Let's say you're taking a break to run for judge. You're elected, but you spend only one term on the bench. In this case, when you rejoin the firm, do you lose all those years of credit or not? Negotiate. Or hire an agent to negotiate for you. Remember that you get what you settle for, and that the negotiation should always result in a win/win. Your plan is to join this group of lawyers and work effectively with them. Neither of you will be able to practice together well if either of you is feeling shortchanged. Resentment will fester, and in stressful times may derail the union.

But if you took your break without making a plan for reentry, don't despair. Simply start right now. Don't spend any more time wondering about whether returning to work is a good thing to do or not. Just get started with your reentry plan. You can adjust as you go if you change your mind. If you left your last practice without a plan to reenter, that doesn't mean you can't rejoin that practice now. Assuming they liked you and valued your work, and assuming they have a place in the practice for a person with your skill set, they will likely welcome you back. As I mentioned earlier, and despite economic downturns, law practices are bleeding experienced lawyers and hiring more laterals than ever before to replace them. You have an advantage because everyone would rather bet on the horse they know than the one they don't.

Statistics suggest, however, that fewer than 5 percent of lawyers taking an extended break want to return to the practices they left. Sometimes, the lawyer was dissatisfied with the practice and doesn't want to return. Sometimes, the practice was dissatisfied with the lawyer and doesn't want him or her on board again. Beyond an unhappy work divorce, certain characteristics of the prior employment may make it an undesirable reentry point, such as an interest in working in a different specialty or on the opposite side of litigation or transactions. Still, going back to the prior practice is the simplest first step because it's the easiest, quickest, and least threatening thing to do. Again, statistics are your friend here. A person who knows you and has worked with you before is five times more likely to hire you than a person who hasn't. You can always move on from that first reentry job if it turns out not to be what you wanted, remember?

Whether you made a plan to rejoin your prior employer before your break or not, it is likely that you will be looking for a new position upon reentry. The most effective approach to this is to treat the reentry job you're seeking as a desirable client you're courting. Strategize the best way to entice the client to hire you. Create a plan and follow through. Begin with understanding the potential client thoroughly. Then, find someone you know or with whom you can easily connect who is familiar with the practice but doesn't work there. Schedule an informational interview with that person and learn as much of the inside baseball about the prospective practice as possible.

If your information gathering confirms that you might like to join that practice, then ask yourself "Why would they hire me?" In other words, what is it that you can contribute to the practice that they would buy in a hot New York minute? Do you have a book of business, a specialty area of practice, a reputation for excellence, or potential rainmaking capacity you can exploit? You may need to do several informational interviews before you recognize your value-added potential to the practice. You may also need to develop that value before you begin the process of interviewing for the position you seek.

Finally, find an advocate inside the organization to help you make the best first connection and make the most of it. At this point you should have enough information to use your precise-visualization techniques in preparation for the interview. These techniques will at least reduce the stress you'll feel during the interview and may make you more likely to negotiate a position you'll love.

Remember that law practices do not hire lawyers on the spot. Connecting well with a new practice is a process that can extend over several months. Lawyers are cautious by nature and will want to fully digest your candidacy before making a decision. Be patient. Have more than one possible employer involved in some stage of the job hunting process at all times. Rejections are inevitable, and you don't want to start over again at the end of a long but unsuccessful courting process. In other words, don't serially job hunt. Instead, keep multiple options on the table at all times.

PowerPlay: Experts agree that the ideal solution is to develop a long-term relationship with one employer, investing at least five years of employment up front before your break and negotiating your return before you leave.

PlugIn: Stay connected to your employer, colleagues, and other alumni groups. If you've allowed too much time between contacts, resume now.

Recommended Resources: *Secrets of Six-Figure Women*, by Barbara Stanny (Harper Business, 2004); *Back on the Career Track*, by Carol Fishman Cohen and Vivian Steir Rabin (Business Plus, 2007).

Best Fresh Tip: Develop the skills necessary to find appropriate mentors for your current situation. Mentors are more important to your long-term career success than any other single factor.

CHAPTER 9

Reentry Points

Lawyers often leave their practices because they believe empowerment is too slow in coming. Or they feel owning power and authority is inconsistent with a fulfilling professional life. Or they fear they can't succeed in the law practice environment because it's too much of an uphill climb. Or they perceive an unspoken policy on work-life balance that is incompatible with their personal goals. These perceptions may color your decision to reenter the workforce as well.

Strategy is required. Before you can begin to find the best point of reentry, you must decide the essential nature of the work and workplace you want and why. The more specific you can be, the more likely you are to find something suitable to your present needs simply because you can easily rule out what you know you don't want and focus your efforts more effectively.

As a consultant, I am often asked to help law practices increase their recruiting and retention success. From such experiences along with my work with individual lawyers, I've learned that practices need good lawyers more than good lawyers need jobs. While job hunting isn't always pleasant, realizing one's worth places the power of reentry right where it should be: with the individual lawyer. Most law practices today are well aware of the competition for recruiting top talent. Over time, practices have developed various strategies for hiring the best possible candidates from among the field of law students and judicial clerks available to them at the entry level. Practices face a considerably greater challenge in retaining good lawyers once they've joined the firm. Either expressly or implicitly, law groups of more than twenty-five lawyers have implemented policies and procedures intended to keep the keepers, with varying levels of short-term success. Many firms have figured out the high cost of attrition, and others have the vague feeling that attrition is costing more than it should but haven't gathered the data necessary to evaluate their own precise costs. Despite the oft-repeated phrase that "the practice of law is a business," many law practices are unable or unwilling to calculate and evaluate the soaring costs of attrition. Firms with more than one hundred lawyers and multiple offices sometimes handle this essential accounting using nothing more than the SWAG method.

Available estimates of the cost of attrition vary from $50,000 to $350,000 or more for each associate lost. When senior associates and all levels of partners leave their firms, costs can be (and usually are) much higher. Over five years, costs per departing lawyer can exceed a million dollars in lost revenue and lost profits as well as the soft costs associated with low morale, lost client relationships, and lost institutional knowledge.

Beyond the hard dollar and soft dollar costs, though, the process of replacing lawyers is exhausting. Recruiting partners begin to feel like Sisyphus, constantly rolling the ball up the hill only to have it roll back down and crush them in the process. Often, hiring partners wail, "What do lawyers want?" By which they mean that lawyers are impossible to please, their demands are unfathomable, and the problem of lawyer attrition is irresolvable no matter how hard they try to fix it. In times of pressing workloads, firms become overwhelmed by their lack of retention success. When the economy is soft, firms cut back on hiring or even lay off lawyers because work slows down, thus increasing the effect of high attrition: fewer lawyers employed means they can't afford to lose any. Yet, when the economy turns around, the good lawyers they want to keep are always the first to leave because good lawyers have more options.

Thus, many mid-sized to smaller firms have simply given up the effort to keep lawyers happy, and changed their business model, downsizing their growth goals. Large firms continue the struggle because significant numbers of lawyers on the payroll are essential to service the clients and industries they desire, but their results are unspectacular. Firms realize that large-scale success is impossible without good lawyers to do the work, which leads to the acquisition of existing practices to build their cadre of producers. Buying lawyers and clients in this way is expensive, and the retention success rate is spotty. Cultures clash. Clients rebel. Lawyers leave.

Modern lawyers feel work should not be a dreaded chore but a stimulating growth opportunity. Ten years ago, I traveled the country presenting to a mostly unreceptive audience the message that lawyer retention depends on job satisfaction. These days, most lawyers and their practices at least recognize that job satisfaction is an essential nonnegotiable baseline for all lawyers, but they are rarely able to translate the desire into reality. Enlightened firms have finally acknowledged that they can only thrive by providing an environment where lawyers can achieve career success. But their efforts to reach this goal have not eliminated their attrition problems. Most programs have failed. This is not the reentry lawyer's problem, but it does present her with significant opportunity.

Lawyers need to develop a career's sturdy three-legged stool: producing great work (which is a matter of professional competence, training, and pride), having great work to do (which means a commitment to rainmaking and training), and enjoying the job. Thus, the question of what lawyers want is not merely the lament of firm administrators, but rather the central question for any individual lawyer considering reentry: What do you want this next phase of your career to be and how are you going to make that happen? Upon this question you must expend a significant number of brain cells (don't worry, you'll make more).

Do you want a full-time legal job in a big law firm with all of its advantages and pitfalls? Do you want a part-time legal job in any law firm, although part-time pay often doesn't mean fewer hours worked? Do you want to be your own boss and can you make a go of it if you go solo? Is flexibility more important to you than status, quality of work, or income? Speaking of income, how much money do you need or want to make? Are you willing to move to a new city? A new region of the country? Abroad?

What kind of work do you want to do, and how do you know? Do you have the requisite expertise for that work or is it something you'll need to develop? If you need to develop new skills, should you do that before you get the job or rely on the practice to train you?

Do you want a legal job at all, or would you rather do something else entirely?

There are many more questions like these you should consider in the contemplation and preparation stages before you decide on the next phase of your career. You don't have to answer all the questions all at once. Take your time. Relax. Think about it a while. Take notes. Keep a journal. This isn't a race. While you will need to create and implement an action plan, acting without clear direction and preparation is at best wasted effort. Even worse, you could be successful in getting a new role you don't really want resulting in another job full of anxiety and dissatisfaction.

The easiest way to find the answers to such questions is to make a game of it. Make this grail something you enjoy seeking. The results of your quest will be truer, and come faster, if you let fun be your guide. Do you doubt it? How long have you been putting off those noxious chores you dread like cleaning the oven or going through your old accounting records stuffed into that shoebox in the back of your closet? 'Nuff said.

For at least a week or two, early in the morning or late at night when its quiet and you're alone, grab a cup of whatever you enjoy, settle into a favorite chair, pick up your favorite pen, play soothing baroque music to stimulate your creative brain, and write down what comes to you, judging nothing, just making a list of, oh, twenty to fifty responses to each question you ask yourself, starting with the ones listed above. Don't think too hard. This is supposed to be easy. All we want to discover at this point is what you believe would suit you best now. The things you write down last are usually the truest.

Begin here: Why would it be fun to get back to work?

PowerPlay: Recognize this journey is an opportunity to improve your life, not a chore. Use the power of precise visualization to secure an Olympic gold medal in job satisfaction. See your new job as a done deal and feel its impact on your life. Lest this seem a bit too new age for lawyers, realize that you need to know what you're seeking before you can recognize it, know where to look for it or grab it when you find it.

PlugIn: Use a journal to tap into your subconscious for answers. Writing your way from here to there is one of the most reliable methods for uncovering a successful reentry target. Little things mean a great deal more than you might at first believe. Annoyances add up and can become too burdensome. Try on your new job and see if you like it before you expend any shoe leather. What do you feel when you think of your new job? What do you look like while you're doing it? What do the offices smell like? What's the view outside your window? Who are your clients? Why do they need you? Why are you the perfect lawyer for them? Why is this job perfect for you now?

Recommended Resources: ConnectWell Consulting's *Journal Your Way There* classes, http://www.connectwellconsulting.com/; *Keeping a Journal You Love*, by Sheila Bender (Walking Stick Press, 2001).

Best Fresh Tip: Make job satisfaction your first goal. This means going after personal happiness first, not expecting happiness to come to you as a reward for selfless service and sacrifice. Well-satisfied lawyers report their priorities in this order:

- Self, family, colleagues, and mentors
- Workplace flexibility
- Personal control over most aspects of the job
- Freedom to design a satisfying career
- Compensation

CHAPTER 10

Money Trips

Financial issues, believe it or not, aren't the most important reasons that people work. Studies of lottery winners repeatedly demonstrate that people work even when they don't need to pay the rent or put food on the table. This is especially true for lawyers, who often are compensated well beyond their immediate needs.

Why do people work, then? The answers are those you would probably give to the same survey question. Eight out of ten people say they would continue working even if they were financially independent. They seek a sense of service, to help themselves and others grow, and to perfect their skills.

But respondents also say they would modify their work to serve their spiritual, social, and artistic values. This suggests that most Americans still view work as a four-letter word. Importantly, the best lawyers do not view work as drudgery or penance to be endured, but rather as a satisfying way to contribute their talents and live a full life.

Research confirms that the best lawyers, those who are high value-added individuals or difficult to replace, are also the happiest lawyers and often the most financially solvent. Make it a goal to become a Platinum Practice™ lawyer and enjoy these common characteristics:

- Exceptionally successful
- Engaged in long-term relationships, in work and in life
- Experts in their chosen field
- Epitomize professionalism
- Have had varied and high-quality experience
- Easy to deal with

If making money is not necessary for you, your best option may be to return to work as a volunteer in a worthy organization. Volunteering is the perfect solution for part-time work. Properly selected volunteer work is a resumé builder and an effective method to increase the quality and level of your personal contact network. Volunteering can also be a more personally rewarding experience. Volunteers are appreciated by their coworkers and the organizations for which they work. It's somewhat easier to leave a volunteer job, you may feel less guilty at taking time off for other pursuits, and the schedule is more flexible. It's a good way to ease into a return to active employment, especially after a long break. You can also try on a few different volunteer jobs and organizations, giving yourself a chance to experiment without causing harm to your resumé or your energy. Remember, though, that nonprofit is a tax status, not a business philosophy. Most nonprofits are operating with a sharp focus on generating revenue, a fact that can work to your advantage in resumé building.

For other lawyers seeking reentry, financial reward will be the primary motivator. Most people do have to earn a living for themselves and their families. Some jobs provide more money than others. High-paying jobs are not necessarily the ones that are the hardest to obtain. Remember that money is what you get in exchange for your energy and talent. The more money you want, the more of your time, energy, and talent you will need to exchange. Money is also a subject fraught with ego reward, which can be the berries or the raspberries. At entry levels, most similarly situated law practices pay salaries in line with their competitors. As lawyers gain experience, their salaries vary widely from one practice to the next based on perceived (not necessarily true) contributions. In many large law firms, corporations, and agencies, salaries are a set range commensurate with experience levels.

If your ego requires a certain salary to support your decision to return to work, you will need to find out how to obtain that salary in the work environment you choose. Your journal can help you here, too. A great plan takes a while to create. For example, if you were a large-firm associate with four years in practice when you took a break to climb Mt. Everest, now seeking to return to the same firm in the same city after two years off, what salary do you want to receive? Most lawyers realize they can't expect to come back into any firm at the same compensation level they would have served if they'd never taken a time-out.

You may be shocked to realize you're expected to pay a penalty greater the two-year leave in salary, benefits, status, opportunity for promotion, and so forth. This is particularly true of organizations providing compensation based on classes or levels of experience. Our hypothetical mountain climber might have to take greater than a two-year hit in his employment level when he returns to work at big law or corporate law or even government law. This is a bitter pill for many lawyers to swallow. The good news is that our hypothetical lawyer is capable of higher-level work and will excel beyond this initial hiring position quickly. The bad news is that many firms with a "level" policy will not increase the lawyer to higher status and compensation levels as quickly as he excels. Depending on their internal policies, the firm may never allow our mountain climber to catch up that salary setback.

Returning part-time to any law firm environment is more difficult than returning full-time, but neither is impossible. Money issues for part-time work are also more complicated. Generally, part-time work does not pay as well as a straight mathematical calculation would suggest. If money is an issue, and part-time is the work you desire for reentry, be prepared to work more than you wish and for less money than might seem fair in most law-firm settings. In corporate and government settings, pay scales for part-time work are somewhat more equitable. Small practices are more part-time friendly than large practices, too.

Finally, some lawyers argue with themselves over the cost of returning to work in light of the financial rewards they believe are feasible. There is no question that it costs money to make money. A sharp pencil and serious number crunching may be necessary to figure out whether returning to work is financially worthwhile at this time. Child-care expenses, for example, may be substantial for toddlers. Commuting costs may require capital investment in a vehicle, and wardrobes updated. Each of these areas must be analyzed on an individual basis to determine the value of a return to work, and which jobs are feasible under the circumstances.

In any case, pull out your journal. These are some of the relevant questions you should answer:

How much money do you need to make? Several hours of studying the household budget may be required. If you need to earn maximum money for minimum time spent at work, consider bonus work such as contingent or fee-premium matters. If only a specific, limited amount of time away from home is available to you now, consider an hourly agreement. Financial considerations may determine whether you can accept a government or corporate job. Be aware that some of these positions require just as many work hours as private practice and sometimes more. Such jobs can also pay considerably less. But you can often get better health care and other benefits in a large corporation or government agency than from a law firm, even if you work part-time. Specialty practices can generate fee premiums which should mean higher compensation. Negotiation is required. Entry-level lawyers are often overpaid for their contributions to the practice. As a reentry or lateral candidate, you will be paid no more than your economic value, but you may be paid less unless you negotiate well. If you aren't a good negotiator on your own behalf, hire an agent to negotiate for you, or at least to coach you on the negotiations.

How tightly is your ego tethered to the money decision? It's essential that you be paid what you are worth. Discounting yourself financially is never a good long-term strategy. It always results in dissatisfaction and leads to serious health and burnout issues.

However, if you feel you're worth more than the job pays, analyze that belief carefully to be sure your money ego isn't artificially inflated. For example, if you've been out of the workforce for two years and seek to reenter a large law firm, regardless of what you've been doing in your absence, the firm will not pay you the same as if you had never left and will most likely pay you significantly less. Or, if a small practice is paid a low hourly rate by its clients, the partners will not view you as worth more than they can afford.

What does your time away from home cost? Stay-at-home parents who return to work must generally incur child-care expenses and other costs associated with reentry. If your profit after taxes is at or near the cost of child-care and other necessary work expenses, you must decide whether returning to work at this time is worthwhile for you and your family. Be sure to include intangible costs in your analysis. Only you can judge how much money will compensate you for time away from your family.

Why are you returning to work? People work for many reasons, only one of which is compensation. Unless returning to work is something you want to do, you're likely to be miserable once you get back into the job.

One final caveat: law firms, departments, and agencies hire the same way many people shop for high-ticket items. First, they decide what they want. Then, they go looking for the right fit. If you're interviewing for a job in a law firm, chances are you won't get it unless you are the square peg they're seeking for that square hole. Assuming you feel you need to be hired, the best advice here is: get the job. Spend a year or more showing them what you can do. Then ask for concessions later if you still need to do so.

PowerPlay: Become a best lawyer to obtain the highest possible levels of job satisfaction and the most appropriate compensation. Go after the best lawyer characteristics directly.

PlugIn: Make peace with money as an exchange of energy for dollars. What do you bring to the table? Be sure you get adequately compensated for your contribution. Identify your value to yourself, your family, and your work in dollars and cents to determine whether you need a paying job or not and to set appropriate salary goals for reentry.

Recommended Resources: *Your Money or Your Life: 9 Steps to Transforming Your Relationship with Money and Achieving Financial Independence: Revised and Updated for the 21st Century,* by Joe Dominguez and Vicki Robin (Penguin, 2008); *Getting A Life,* by Jacqueline Blix and David Heitmiller (Viking, 1997).

Best Fresh Tip: Corporations don't often hire entry-level lawyers, which means you'll have an experience advantage if you choose to apply. Be realistic about your compensation prospects, neither over- nor underestimating your value. Accurate data about compensation is difficult to find because compensation ranges for lawyers vary widely due to subjective and objective factors. Recruiters often possess salary information they are willing to share without identifying the specific private employer. Government agency, law school, and corporation salaries for lawyers can be obtained online. Check, e.g., information.com for law firm salaries; and *Law Department Compensation Benchmarking Survey,* published annually by Altman Weil, Inc., at http://www.altmanweil.com. For government agency salaries, you can contact the agency directly or the relevant bar association.

CHAPTER 11

Navigating Reentry

Once you've decided to reenter the workforce, how do you find the right opportunity? There are many sources of assistance and advice available for job hunters of all persuasions. In addition, an entire reentry industry has sprung up around the issue of women who take a break from working to have and raise children. The amount of information out there, online and in the bookstores and elsewhere, is overwhelming. Most of it is very negative. Beware: Choice fatigue and despair can set in rapidly if you head out on this path. A better approach is to keep your reentry as simple and easy as possible.

When I interviewed for my first job out of law school, one aspect of the search terrified me more than any other. I believed I was making a lifelong decision. I thought I would have only one chance to choose the law practice where I would spend my entire forty-year career. Making a mistake seemed fatal. Back then, I was almost right. When I read *The Firm*, the best-selling novel by John Grisham, I thought he had it right. His character literally made a deal with the devil by taking a job that was too good to be true; the only way out was death. There was a time when lawyers spent their entire careers with one firm, or in one corporate job, or in one government agency. That time is not now. As I mentioned in Chapter 7, more than 80 percent of new hires have left their first jobs in the first five years, which is double the rate of attrition ten years ago. Four years is the average length of stay in any corporate job, regardless of experience level or job title.

It should be comforting to know that you don't have to make the one and only eternal best choice for your first reentry position. Crystal balls are rare. No one can predict the future. If you are a woman, statistics suggest you will take at least four off-ramp detours during your career. For men, the statistical number is three.

Take the pressure off. Realize that even if you do love it, chances are your new job will not be 'til death. Indeed, it's unlikely to be more than a two- to four-year commitment, under the best of circumstances. Unlike Grisham's Mitch McDeere, you're not signing your life away and you can leave any time you choose. This means you can try something on and see how you like it. If you don't like the job, you can change it. If they don't like you, they can fire you. No one is shackled to the desk. This is an extremely liberating fact. Embrace it and you will flash freeze your lawyerly tendency to analysis paralysis. So first, realize that you only have to make one easy choice based on what you know and want right now. You don't have to foresee and predict the future, or cover all the risks the future might present. You can ease into things now and make adjustments as necessary.

Also realize that job-hunting books or professionals may not be the help you need for several reasons. Perhaps the most important is the negative approach these resources take to attacking the hunt and landing a new job. The assumption with which most job-hunting advice begins is that the job is something for which you should change or adapt who you are and what you want from life in order to be chosen by the employer. If you're over forty, you'll be advised to stress your youthful characteristics to avoid age discrimination. If you're female, you'll be warned about sex discrimination. If you're a parent, you'll be told not to talk about your kids during interviews lest you appear frivolous and not seriously committed to the work. If you've made a lot of money in the past, you'll be given strategies to respond to "Why are you willing to take a pay cut to work here?" questions. And so forth. This approach, and the underlying assumptions upon which it is based, contains kernels of wisdom, but it is depressing and debilitating. Not to mention unnecessary. Don't fall for it. While job hunting may not be as much fun as an afternoon at the beach, you're not trolling for a handout, either.

Instead, realize that you are the golden goose. You are the one with the license to practice law, the ability to generate income for the practice, and the desire to contribute your talents to the job. You are not a beggar. You do not have your hat in hand. Or, if you feel you are begging, you need some self-esteem building before you head out on this particular daring adventure. If you are seeking to reenter the work world, that means you have been employed in the past. Real confidence comes from competence coupled with experience of success. While job hunting, false confidence works just as well as the real thing. Act confident whether you are or not. Realize that attractive people (meaning people who are attractive in this particular job interview) are perceived as more competent, so dress and groom yourself appropriately. Likeable people are also perceived as more successful, so project a competent, accomplished demeanor. In short, fake it 'til you make it.

Let's look at the resources that might seem like the solutions to finding the perfect reentry position:

You'll be tempted to start with recruiters. But head-hunting agencies are an especially poor place to seek your future because recruiters are hired by law practices to find the right square peg candidate for the square hole the practice has already identified. If you're a square peg, you may get an interview. Otherwise, you won't. Recruiters do not provide career counseling or help you find a job. That's simply not their role. You should contact recruiters and allow them to send you on interviews if that suits your needs, but don't rely on them as your only source of potential employment.

The American Bar Association does not have any services to assist you with reentry except this book. It is unlikely your state or local bar association provides such services either. While this may change in the future, for now, bar associations are not useful resources for reentry seekers.

Law schools do have placement offices and some assist with alumni placement needs. Check with your alma matter, but it's unlikely you will find an appropriate reentry job through your law school placement office. Not because they are unwilling to help you, but because the number of jobs they have available is limited.

Private industry has attempted to fill this gap, and some companies are well worth contacting. A plethora of reentry consultants are easily identifiable with a quick-and-dirty Internet search. Look at them. Interview a few. Perhaps you'll find one or more that suits your needs.

Temporary agencies flourish in the legal world now, providing contract lawyers to many law practices. Do consider these. If you are seeking part-time work only, this may be your easiest, quickest, most flexible option. Agencies can also assist with temp-to-perm situations, giving you a chance to try on a job before you commit to it. These agencies are good alternatives for finding jobs in nonlegal fields, too, if you decide to go that route.

Agencies will not be the most lucrative option for the individual lawyer, even for part-time work. Agencies take a portion of the fees paid by the employers they service. If you would like to do full- or part-time contract legal work, the most lucrative way to do that is to find your own work and retain the entire fee paid by the practice. You will need to become thoroughly familiar with your state bar's rules governing contract lawyers. You may also need to buy your own malpractice insurance. You'll need a contract, a place to work, and a method for billing and collecting your fees.

By far the best resource to assist you with your reentry is your network, both on and off the internet. Research has consistently confirmed for more than twenty-five years that more jobs are obtained through networking than any other single method and by all the other methods combined. Why? Because when people know you, or know someone who knows you, they feel more comfortable about hiring you. This should not be a surprise; the same dynamic is present when clients engage you to perform legal work or when you hire anyone to do anything for yourself.

What may be a surprise is that most jobs are found through your network's weak ties, not your strong ties. This is true because people in your closest circles tend to know the same people and be aware of the same opportunities. They would have already helped you to find work before you bought this book. But people to whom you are more tenuously connected have wider circles of influence that you haven't tapped into yet.

What are the actual statistics? The numbers vary (which is one of the reasons the U.S. government reports unemployment numbers every month) and are not specific to lawyers. Internet job searches are successful less than 10 percent of the time. Sending out random resumés works about 7 percent of the time, as does answering ads in professional journals and local newspapers. Private employment agencies produce somewhat better results, particularly for women, about 28 percent of whom find new jobs this way. Seeking a job by asking your strong ties for leads results in about a 33 percent success rate. Cold call contacts followed by a personal face-to-face meeting generate about 70 percent of new jobs, and doing this with a couple of colleagues who are also looking has a slightly higher success rate of 84 percent.

Your task, and it's not mission impossible, is to demonstrate to the practice with which you want to work that you will add value to their organization, which will benefit from your work. Make them want you, yes, but not because you're their perfect square peg. Instead, they should want you because you bring something to the table that's desirable to them. Your task is to figure out what it is that you have to offer and present your assets appropriately so that they don't miss the point. No one gambles on a lawyer who might be good enough. Everyone buys a sure-thing contributor.

PowerPlay: Begin creating a great plan for reentry designed to go directly for the job you want. The plan may require initial employment in a short-term job to gain experience in a particular field or additional training before moving up to the job you're seeking.

PlugIn: Be strategic in your reentry plan to avoid choice fatigue and paralysis by analysis caused by the overwhelming number of options available to today's job seekers. Don't get swamped by dismal statistics and horror stories. Stay focused on creating and working your plan.

Recommended Resources: *What Color Is Your Parachute*, by Richard Nelson Bolles (Ten Speed Press). This classic job-hunter's guide is revised each year and includes step-by-step instructions for finding a job. Not all apply to lawyers, but Bolles takes the mystery out of the process.

Best Fresh Tip: A few universities, businesses, and bar associations offer seminars and classes to assist you with preparations to reenter the workforce. Use these if you feel the need, but make the most of the opportunity by networking effectively before, during, and after the seminars.

CHAPTER 12

Navigating Reentry into Large Law Firms

Large law firms are the most visible and prevalent legal employers. More lawyers work for large firms than any other type of employer, followed by government (state and federal), mid-sized and small law firms, corporations (for profit and nonprofit), other professional firms (accounting, brokerage) and associations, solo practices, and temporary contract agencies.

Returning to legal work generally involves at least a passing consideration of seeking a job with a large law firm, particularly if you've previously worked in a large law firm practice. Do not discount large firms simply because you've acquired a negative impression of them. Investigate the particular firms you're interested in thoroughly. I've worked in and with large firms for most of my years in practice. They vary widely, as do the lawyers who practice within them. Large firms present some of the most exciting opportunities for lawyers available today. For the right lawyers, large firms can be the best practice environments.

Whether you've worked in a large firm or not, you should first acquire as clear a picture as possible of the work environment for the firms you're considering. Begin with the firm's Web site for a complete overview of the practice, its attorneys and offices, recent matters, awards and recognition, charitable and bar activities, history, and representative clients. You may find pictures of their offices around the country and the world and candid pictures of the people who work in them. Also posted will be recruiting practices aimed at entry-level lawyers and, in some cases, lateral lawyers. You won't find salaries posted on the Web site, but the firm will post other employment benefits. What firm policies matter to you?

This initial Web site analysis will give you a brief overview of the firm. If you're still interested, do a bit more research on their Web site. Go back to those candid pictures. How are the lawyers dressed? Is the atmosphere formal, informal, casual? Check out the attorneys in the offices where you are interested in working. How many lawyers work in that office? Enough to provide you with the collegiality, training, support, and client-referral opportunities you need? Which practice groups are located there? Will those practices complement your work? Will you be able to build your practice and your skills there?

How many attorneys are men, women, associates, partners? Are there attorneys of color? Where did these lawyers go to law school? How long have they been with the firm? If they came to the firm from other jobs, what were those jobs? A significant element of lawyer job satisfaction is a working environment including colleagues you like. How many attorneys in the office you're investigating are similar to you? How many seem like people with whom you'd enjoy working?

After this initial research, use precise visualization to check your gut feelings about the place. Still good? Then keep this one on your list of possible reentry targets. Make a note of anyone you know in the firm, any client listed that you're familiar with, anyone who has a connection to something or someone that you might be able to connect to once you begin to work your reentry plan. Do the same research for any other large firms that interest you.

Next, use the Internet to investigate other aspects of large law firms. Simply entering the names of the firms you've chosen into a search engine like Google will bring up a great deal of information. You're looking for articles about working at these firms. You want to know whether the lawyers already employed there are satisfied with the firm or not, and why or why not.

You may find fairly dismal statistical information about large firms in general. As I've already mentioned, large firms have high attrition rates among lawyers. They are also criticized for poor track records on advancing women and minorities. Large firms generally bill clients by the hour, and the number of hours attorneys are expected to bill can be substantial. Often, large firms have clients around the country and the world, so business travel may be required. It is important to keep in mind that general statistics and anecdotal information may not apply to any particular firm or to you individually. The atmosphere in various practice groups and offices within large firms is a better indicator of most aspects of a lawyer's daily life and is something that varies widely. Another important factor is your unique character. One lawyer's reaction to perceived negative micro-messages may be quite different from another's. Your ambitions, talents, and abilities as well as your individualized approach to your work can significantly alter your views.

Large firms perform sophisticated legal work for sophisticated clients. The quality level of work and clients can be far higher than smaller firms, corporations, or government. The clients can have higher expectations of their lawyers and the legal work those lawyers perform. Fees charged for the work are generally higher than in smaller firms, and junior lawyer salaries can be higher than in smaller firms, corporations, or government agencies. Thus, the pressure to perform at higher levels may be substantial, but so are the rewards.

Your efforts to reenter a large firm are most likely to succeed if you begin with reasonable expectations. Law practices of all types are businesses with a profit motive. Thus, the first question is: what business value will you bring to the practice? In today's world, legal skills and a willingness to work are the entry-level requirements only for law students seeking their first jobs. Most employers require much more from reentry lawyers, particularly more senior reentry candidates. Large firms may have enough work to support lawyers with no particular specialty or portable business. Those jobs are usually specifically defined by the firm or a practice area within the firm. A recruiter may be hired to locate the right person for the job. If you have contacted recruiters and placed your resumé with them, you could be one of the lawyers considered for the position. Or you may be interviewed if you've made your interest in the position known to the firm through your network.

In private practice firms, reentry and lateral lawyers usually seek demonstrated rainmaking ability, a portable book of business, or a specialized skill set that the firm needs and is willing to pay for in the absence of a portable book of business.

One exception to this general rule is alumni of particular mid- to large-sized firms. Even if you left a mid- to large-sized firm with no formal reentry programs in place, you should check back when you're ready to consider reentry. If you had a mentor at the firm, contact him or her first. Assuming you were a great lawyer when you left, they'll want you back. Things have changed in the practice while you've been away. You may find you like the firm even better than you did before.

PowerPlay: Large law firms present challenges for reentering lawyers, but also significant potential. Find as many connections between you and the firm as possible. Create a strategic plan for approaching and joining the firm.

PlugIn: Ignore the negative and stay focused on the positive aspects of large firm practice. Take personal responsibility for creating a successful career within the realities.

Recommended Resources: See http://backonthecareertrack.com/, a Web site devoted to stay-at-home moms who want to return to work and also to relaunchers, which they define as people who build a career, then take a break, and seek to return.

Best Fresh Tip: Consider alumni associations (law school, college, high school, past employers); better yet, start an alumni association using the Internet. Contact connectwell.com for our white paper on creating a powerful alumni group.

CHAPTER 13

Ramping Up

It should go without saying that you cannot practice law without an active law license. If you have allowed your license to lapse, or have moved from a jurisdiction where you were licensed but now seek to work in a jurisdiction where you are not licensed, the situation will need to be corrected. If possible, you should reinstate your license before you seek work because you'll have more flexibility and control over the opportunities available to you.

There may be a few exceptions to this blanket statement of the obvious in some jurisdictions, but the cracks are closing. For example, in some corporate legal departments or government agency positions, you are not required to be licensed in the state where the job is located. This is usually a matter of law, although corporate or agency policies may also exist. Requirements vary by jurisdiction. Generally, it is not sufficient to be admitted in one state and plan to practice only in Federal Court in a state where you are not licensed. Nor is it a long-term solution to assume you won't be required to appear in court, or can be admitted to cases pro hac vice, or can simply co-counsel without formal appearance if you have a licensed lawyer on the case.

If you have allowed your law license to lapse, the best course is to do what you need to do to become active again before seeking work. The second best course is to begin the process for renewing your license before you interview. The third best course is to get a stopgap job or take a volunteer position while you bring your license up to date.

Perhaps the most significant concern for a licensed lawyer returning to law practice is making sure your substantive skills are up to the work you will be expected to perform. Returning to an established law practice will be much more likely and satisfying if you can hit the ground running. For your first job out of law school, you were expected to be inexperienced and only to know how to think like a lawyer; the practice was prepared to train you. This time, you will be hired based on what you can already do, not on what you might be able to learn.

There have been substantial changes in many areas of law in the past five years, and more changes follow almost every legislative session. It is essential that you be ready, willing, and able to practice in your chosen specialty before you attempt to return, or at the very least that you are willing to learn the changes in the law on your own time once you are hired.

This is an ethical issue as well as a practice issue. The ethical rules in all jurisdictions require lawyers to be competent or capable of acquiring competence before accepting representation. In the criminal law arena, ineffective assistance of counsel is a ground for appeal. In civil practice, the specter of malpractice suits looms. Thus, you must commit yourself to developing sufficient legal skills before you accept work. Fortunately, this is usually just a matter of a tune-up in your knowledge, not a need to return to law school and start over. Remember those brain pathways you developed while you were practicing before you took your break? They're still there. You will find that law practice is much like any other skill you've developed. Most of it will come back to you when you start actively focusing again. If you're planning to reenter in a completely different practice area, you may have a longer learning curve on substantive law, but even that learning will be easier than if you'd never practiced any kind of law before.

If you have a gap in your malpractice coverage, you must also deal with that gap. Insurance policies vary, but many carriers will not insure you for a reasonable premium if you have been practicing law but have not had coverage for a period of time. Some carriers will not insure you at all when you've had a gap in coverage.

To find out what changes have occurred and where to find the best education, use your network. Contact a practicing lawyer in your jurisdiction and your area of practice, tell him or her that you're planning to return to practice and ask (a) what changes have occurred since you last practiced, and (b) what is the best way to get up to speed as quickly as possible? Failing a good personal source, contact the chair of the appropriate section of the local or state bar in which you wish to return to practice and conduct an informational interview. The bar association will be glad to help you.

Fortunately, these are all areas where your state or local bar association can help. Continuing Legal Education (CLE) is available either free or at modest cost from every bar association. Often, CLE can be done online or by renting audio or video of the necessary courses. Peruse the online course listings for CLE from your state and local bar associations to get a strong picture of recent developments as well as the knowledge you need to get up to speed.

Sometimes the best source of quick-and-dirty practical education is found in bar review course materials. These materials focus on minimal levels of competence necessary to pass the various bar exams and spend very little time on philosophy or hypothetical instances. You can find them online or through your bar association.

In addition to substantive skills, you will need good technology skills. Technology, unlike the practice of law, does change at lightning speed. If you've been away from the practice for more than two years, it is likely that significant changes have occurred, at least in small- to mid-sized law firms and in corporations. Larger firms and government agencies are slower to implement new technology, but an absence of three to five years from the law should guarantee several changes in the use of technology even in those workplaces.

Once again, this is where the nature of the legal business will give you a helping hand. Lawyers and law practices are notoriously slow to acquire and adapt to new technology. While many new software applications are out there and being used on a regular basis by the rest of the world, law practices are not likely to have embraced most of them. Hardware adoptions in law practices are even slower. If you can use a PC, you are likely to be fine in the hardware department. If you're a Mac user, you'll have a few more challenges, but using both PCs and Macs is easier than ever these days. Prior skills will be revived once you begin, and learning new programs will be faster than if you'd never used technology in the past. At a minimum, you should be able to use a smart phone and a computer expertly, know your way around the Internet, be completely capable of creating your own documents in Word, Excel, and PowerPoint, be fluent in computerized legal research techniques, and have at least a passing understanding of online resources such as Lexis-Nexis and digital filing requirements for legal documents.

While some law practices do still have secretaries to handle document creation and editing, many practices now rely on the lawyers themselves to do so. Whether or not you'll have a secretary, there will be many times when you will need to handle things yourself. At a minimum, your confidence will suffer if you feel you must rely on others to do your work for you.

Because Microsoft Office programs are so ubiquitous in our culture, there are many online classes that teach them, resources to help you, and local live classes at various times of the day and night if you prefer the hands-on tutorial method of learning. A Google search for "learn [Word or other program name]" should point you in the right direction and give you more options than you need. Or, Google the Web site for the program and you'll find additional options.

Software updates do have a learning curve, but it's minimal when you've already learned the basics of the software in the past. Updates that claim to be new and improved don't mean "drastically changed and incomprehensible to our current customers who have been using us for years." New law practice-specific software will present your biggest challenge. The good news is that law practices and specialties within practices use different software, and there is no industry standard that is universally applicable everywhere. This means you can learn the appropriate software on the job once you get it; you don't need to go into the job already possessing the genius-level skill you will develop after you start working there.

In addition, procedural rules for maintaining computerized data have changed significantly, and you must develop sufficient knowledge of them to avoid jeopardizing your ability to adequately represent your clients. Serious preventable ethical and legal mistakes have already arisen in cases handled by experienced lawyers who haven't taken a break from practice. Don't let that happen to you. Get the CLE you need to bring yourself up to date by checking your state and local bar association Web sites. Again, you can usually take these classes at home in front of your own computer at your convenience for minimal cost and often for free.

PowerPlay: Be self-sufficient when it comes to office technology to broaden your appeal to law practices of all sizes and increase the job's flexibility to suit your needs. Understand how computers store data to avoid inadvertent disclosure of client-sensitive information.

PlugIn: Buy a smart phone and learn to use it. Use your home computer to your best advantage by learning necessary computer skills before you return to work. Take at least one online CLE course on the new Federal Rules of Civil Procedure governing the handling of electronic data to avoid unwittingly jeopardizing your client's confidential communications and your work-product privilege.

Recommended Resources: *How to Start and Build a Law Practice,* by Jay Foonberg (American Bar Association, 2004); *The Complete Guide to Contract Lawyering: What Every Lawyer and Law Firm Needs to Know About Temporary Legal Service,* by Deborah Arron and Deborah Guyol (Niche Press, 1999); *Technology in the Law Office,* by Thomas F. Goldman (Prentice Hall, 2007).

Best Fresh Tip: Use bar review courses to update your substantive legal skills or learn new areas of the law quickly and accurately.

CHAPTER 14

Work/Life Balance

While you've been on a break, your life has been out of balance because you're out of the workforce. Even though your days are full and you may even feel overwhelmed if you've been engaged in consuming activity, your work/life balance has tipped in the direction of life.

Yet, without meaningful work, most lawyers feel dissatisfied and unfulfilled. Many lawyers who have overemphasized life at the expense of work are suffering stress from financial scarcity. Others miss the challenge of legal work or the camaraderie of like-minded colleagues. Some feel their education is going to waste or their abilities are evaporating with disuse. All of these are symptoms of imbalance between work and life.

After reentry, the pendulum of work/life balance swings toward work. It's too easy to become overwhelmed with the demands of the new job along with the full life you've already created. Moving out of your comfort zone into a new work environment, particularly returning to the practice of law where your service to others is paramount, is stressful. Handling the change will be one of your most significant reentry challenges, followed closely by achieving work/life balance once you're entrenched in your next job. From my own experience and the experience of other lawyers, be reassured that work/life balance is possible and within your grasp.

Frankly, the majority of lawyers enjoy very little work/life balance, but there is hope for improvement. Lack of balance has contributed to burnout, high attrition rates (more than 19 percent flee from the profession as a whole), substance abuse, and depression. The statistics are frightening. Johns Hopkins University reports that lawyers are 3.6 times more likely to experience depression during their careers than any other profession, due in large part to stress and lack of balance. All bar associations have implemented programs to deal with soaring stress-related illnesses among lawyers and have begun emphasizing balance.

One of the reasons lawyers are so highly paid (lawyers fall into the top 1 percent of wage-earners in the United States and by some reports are the highest-paid occupation in the country) is the amount of time and energy we devote to work in exchange for that high compensation. Everyone has the same twenty-four-hour day to allocate. When a disproportionate number of hours are consistently devoted to work at the expense of life and self-care, stress and burnout are inevitable. Don't be fooled. Stress kills.

As a recovering workaholic who has known many similarly afflicted colleagues, I can say unequivocally that work/life balance is completely doable in American law practices—whether the reason for seeking balance is to be with children, or to run marathons and watch sunsets, or to avoid illness and premature death. Because it suits our lawyer personality, the best news is that balance is within your control.

Balance must be an individual goal like other health goals. While lawyers may someday get to the point where balance can be a policy implemented by firms and other organizations, we are clearly not there yet. Nor is there any other industry that promotes balance except perhaps education, where institutions actually close for a certain number of weeks or months each year, forcing educators to take time away from school. Even in education, however, instructors often crowd those empty weeks with additional work and return to their classrooms exhausted.

Achieving work/life balance is every lawyer's personal responsibility. We owe it to our lives and our work and ourselves to master this skill. It's important to realize that balance is not something we have; balance is something we do. Balance is a skill that needs to be learned and practiced constantly. In my seminars, we demonstrate this point with a simple physical-balance test administered by physical trainers. Knowing how to do the test, what the results will be, and what it measures does not affect the validity of the test. In other words, you can't psych-out the result, you can only experience it.

Stand up near something like a chair or a wall in case you fall. Put your hands on your hips. Then lift one leg like a flamingo. You should be able to balance on one leg for at least thirty seconds. Then try the other leg. Then try the exercise with your eyes closed. What you'll notice is that you have to work to keep your balance. You're constantly moving the muscles in your leg to remain balanced. You should be able to balance longer with your eyes open, because you take visual cues from your surroundings. With your eyes closed, balance is harder.

There are several points to be learned from this demonstration. First, knowing about balance is not the same thing as doing it. Second, balance requires constant effort. Third, balance is easier when you can see and are aware of your surroundings. Fourth, balance gets easier with practice. Finally, your brain is involved with balance, but so is your body. Without appropriate conditioning of both brain and body, balance is at least harder to achieve and maintain, and in some cases, it's impossible.

Physical balance is extremely important, and not just for toddlers learning to walk or kids learning to ride a bike. Debilitating falls cause many seniors to die each year. Adults in their prime can be sidelined for months with broken bones or soft tissue injuries when balance is compromised. Certainly being off your feet for weeks or months makes it much more difficult to work or to care for loved ones. Keeping yourself in good physical balance is essential to life itself.

Work/life balance is no less essential if for no other reason than the need to practice and maintain physical balance. Start there if the other motivations for creating and maintaining work/life balance haven't boosted your enthusiasm for developing the necessary skills.

Work/life balance requires giving up some of the tangible and intangible rewards you would get for spending an unbalanced amount of time at work. If there are consequences associated with allocating an appropriate number of hours to work, you simply must decide to accept or endure them.

Achieving balance means you must balance your desire for more work rewards against your need to spend time on yourself, with your family, or on some other project. If you want to work in a traditional law firm practice, you may also sacrifice some money, prestige, and advancement to achieve work/life balance. In my personal experience and the experience of many colleagues, a better balanced life has provided greater financial rewards as well as other rewards. Your balanced life can too. But like physical balance, no one can do it for you.

Visualize a playground teeter-totter. When it is balanced, neither seat is on the ground and neither seat is high in the air. If you choose balance, you won't get as high in the air at equipoise, but neither will you be stuck on the ground.

Single parents and two-working-parent families are common in today's legal workplace. They face additional work/life balance challenges because children who are unable to care for themselves depend on their parents. While many have argued that law practices should change to accommodate parents and their additional challenges, very little change has occurred. To succeed in law practice, parents must learn

65

to manage these challenges. The lawyer personality is perfect for designing solutions to such difficult conundrums.

Lest we think the challenges facing working parents are recent phenomena or somehow peculiar to modern society, they aren't. My grandmother and grandfather worked outside the home for their entire adult lives while raising nine children. Women now over fifty were more often than not working mothers when their children were young. Most men have always been working fathers.

Recall Justice O'Connor's winding road to success, and the many detours she traveled to take care of her family. Think of working mom Justice Ginsberg or former vice-presidential candidate Geraldine Ferraro. Ferraro worked as a second-grade teacher while she pursued a law degree at night. She took a thirteen-year career break to raise her three children. She worked at the Queens County District Attorney's office before her election to the U.S. House of Representatives in 1978 where she served three terms before Walter Mondale selected her as his running mate.

Lawyer Nancy Pelosi, Speaker of the House of Representatives, has five children. Governor Sarah Palin of Alaska, another mother of five, is not a lawyer but she is a former vice-presidential candidate like Ferraro. President Barack Obama and First Lady Michelle Obama are both lawyers and have two daughters. Senator John McCain and his humanitarian wife, Cindy, have seven children between them.

In short, working mothers and working fathers are not a curiosity, but the very fabric of our world. It may be counterintuitive, but the fact is that choosing to have one parent stay home to raise children has always been a luxury that required families to sacrifice money, career advancement, leisure time, clean houses, homemade birthday cakes, and sleep. Today's parents may want to stay home to raise children and surely feel stretched in several different directions as they attempt to do so. But don't be tempted to believe this is a new phenomenon or that it's impossible for you or your family to thrive while you do so. Those mental attitudes are self-defeating and unnecessary.

During my years as a lawyer and consultant to lawyers, I have known many parent lawyers, both male and female. Rearing children, either while practicing law or while taking a break, has been a challenge for all of them in one way or another. If the children have special needs, or there is only one parent in the home, or the income is not sufficient to pay for child care or assistance with homemaking chores, the challenges are greater. How do they do it? Some have no choice. They must work to support or help support themselves and their families. In those cases, believe it or not, working parents do much less hand-wringing and worrying about the situation. Because there seem to be no other options, they simply figure it out and just do it. The successful ones figure out how to have balance in their lives.

However, when lawyers in this situation sacrifice themselves for their children and their work, they reap the health disasters noted earlier. When lawyers do have a choice between working outside the home and staying home with children, they seem to struggle more with that decision. Why? My theory is, again, that we're lawyers. Lawyers worry. That's what we do. We have a pessimism bias, we're trained to analyze risks and avoid them, and we focus on everything that could go wrong. Until we've at least identified all the possible harm, controlled everything we can control, and made our plan Bs for the uncontrollable, we believe there is no safety.

And then there's the guilt. Guilt can be overwhelming when mothers or fathers choose to return to work and leave their children with caretakers—regardless of who those caretakers are and how good a job they do with the children—especially when parents choose to but aren't required to work outside the home.

One working lawyer mother told me, "I always knew that my nanny was doing a much better job than I would have if I was there. That made it easier to go to work. But when the kids were sick, and I was out of town talking to them on the phone and they were crying for Mommy, I won't tell you I felt good about that."

A working father said, "I never get to see my daughter because I travel so much. She's growing up way too fast. I feel like I have to be with her every minute when I am in town, so I have no social life away from her. My relationship with my wife has suffered because of that. She's a lawyer, too, which makes it a little easier. At least we both understand what the workload is like, and neither one of us is guilting the other one for being gone."

Working parents do manage work/life balance when they have demanding roles both in and out of the office. They determine what they must do themselves and delegate the rest. They explain to their kids that people need to work and contribute to the family as well as to the world. They demonstrate that productive men and women get up and go to work, but they also come home and relax with the family, and take care of themselves, too.

Like all lawyers who value work/life balance, working parents make balance a priority. They take care of themselves physically and mentally so that they can perform both work and family projects. Parents limit business travel or take the family along. (One benefit of a lot of business travel is those fat frequent flyer miles accounts and the extra money to take the kids.) They follow a long stint at work on a difficult case or a short-timeline deal by one or a few days off. This is possible if scheduling is totally up to the individual lawyer to handle. One effective strategy is never to allow anyone to put anything on your calendar except you. You are the only one who knows how much you have to accomplish and how much time and energy you will need to devote to every item. Don't let something as simple as calendaring cause any stress in your life.

Efficiency while in the office, fewer chats with coworkers, and leaving the office on time are all within the lawyer's control. Telecommuting can be an essential part of the plan for balance. But double backup child care is a must. Sick children need attention, and the parents can't always be the ones to handle them.

The most successful working parents have the right mind-set, the right relationship with their children and spouses, and the right child care. They constantly remind themselves why they're working and why that choice is the best one for them and their families.

Finally, successful working parents realize they won't be working parents forever. Children become self-sufficient, and they do leave home eventually. Because the stresses of balancing children and work are not permanent, they're bearable. Working parents see light at the end of the tunnel and realize they can make it with a few strategies, the right self-care, appropriate delegation, a good attitude, and a big dose of humor.

Only you know whether you can balance a busy law practice with the rest of your life at this time, or not. Sometimes, lawyers must simply realize that a boss or client who doesn't understand the lawyer's time constraints is not worthy of the lawyer's personal sacrifice. Clients and bosses can be fired, too.

If you can't achieve balance, or don't choose to return to work, then honor your choice. Leave defensiveness behind. Celebrate your decision to spend more time with your family or interests other than your job, for now. Remember, whether to reenter now or not is a decision that can be changed down the road. Fortunately for everyone, reentry isn't a once-in-a-lifetime opportunity. As one client told me, "There's always another bus coming by."

PowerPlay: Don't be dysfunctionally independent. Delegate everything you can delegate and only do what's truly necessary yourself. Err on the side of delegating to allow more time for self-care if family members are well cared for by others.

PlugIn: Keep your own calendar. Do not allow anyone to schedule anything on your calendar without your express consent.

Recommended Resources: Project for Attorney Retention, at http://www.pardc.org/.

Best Fresh Tip: If you want to work balanced hours in your current practice, the key issue is whether supervising attorneys are on board. Help them get there by making a business case for your plan.

CHAPTER 15

Roadblocks for Mothers

Of course, returning to work when one is a mother of young children is no easy task. The difficulties have been well documented in all fields, including the practice of law. One need only look at the dismally low rates at which women actually use the policies existent in law practices meant to provide a parent-friendly workplace to realize what a struggle mothers of young children find with the return to work.

At the same time, millions of mothers achieve this difficult assignment every day and thousands of them are lawyers. We know raising children and practicing law can be successfully done. The question is: how can you do it most effectively for your family?

You will never be comfortable leaving your children for any reason unless you feel 1,000 percent certain that they are well cared for in your absence. This is not an easy feat to manage because it's mostly a mental issue for the mothers, not fact-based reality for the children. Most mothers are ambivalent at best about leaving their children with others. We all know that crying child, clinging to his mommy's neck, begging her to stay and play with him today, will be redirected and laughing less than ten minutes after Mommy leaves for work. Still, it's heart wrenching to see them cry when Mommy wants to stay home today, too.

Child-care problems do exist, and the media is more than willing to exploit the small percentage of real disasters out there. We've all seen the horrifying video from nanny cameras documenting abusive or neglectful nannies, and so forth. We can't ignore potential child safety hazards, but we don't have to let those hazards rule, either. Remember that half a million planes landing safely today is not news. That is, most child-care arrangements lawyer mothers employ work very well. If any valid concerns arise, lawyer mothers make necessary changes.

Fear for our personal safety and the safety of our offspring is an innate human condition. Like most rational fears, it is well grounded in reality. We cannot do our best, let alone thrive, if our physical, mental, or emotional selves are truly unsafe. Making sure your children are well cared for in your absence is nonnegotiable. That said, parents are of less value to their children if the parent is unable to provide basic sustenance, including not only food and shelter, but emotional and psychological support, health care, social training, and the other essential aspects of parenthood. The best illustration of this point is the instruction we've all heard hundreds of times on plane flights: put on your own oxygen mask first, and then assist small children or others. Without oxygen, we can help no one, including ourselves.

Moms often worry that they have lost their mental acuity for work, lost their edge. The truth is everyone feels rusty after an extended break from work. Women tend to internalize their work problems, and men tend to externalize. In other words, women tend to think they have made a mistake whereas men blame external factors for mistakes. Moms sometimes take this a step further and assume they are not capable of returning to work successfully. Yet researchers have shown that motherhood enhances brainpower in several areas, including perception, motivation, efficiency, resiliency, and essential emotional intelligence. For more information on this subject, read Katherine Ellison's *The Mommy Brain: How Motherhood Makes Us Smarter* (Basic Books, 2006).

When mothers return to work in a law practice, they are not different from other lawyers as much as similar to them. Indeed, these days the lawyer without children is more unusual than the lawyer with children. You should not consider yourself an outsider because you won't be one. There are challenges for parents who desire to participate in an active full-time law practice, of course. The fallacy is believing that no one else faces similar, equal, or greater challenges. Navigating challenges is the essence of life as well as work. Accepting this may mean taking off the blinders you've been wearing while spending time in what one woman called "the baby tunnel." In other words, thinking that everything revolves around your child and your relationship to your child at times when that one-pointed focus is not really required.

As one lawyer mother of two college graduates explained the irony, "When they're babies, you want to be with them because they seem so helpless and the truth is that they don't need you there. Any competent caregiver will do a good job. When they're teens, you don't want to be with them because they are so difficult, and that's when they really do need you there, but they won't let you near them."

Perhaps the most essential skill for working mothers to master is developing necessary boundaries. Like any skill, this one requires practice and experience. Technology helps and hinders. Constant accessibility via cell phones has eliminated parental concerns about being out of touch with the kids or their caretakers, but can tether parents inappropriately to a cellular umbilical cord. Successful working parents schedule time to talk to the kids and caretakers on the phone. Otherwise, they enforce rules limiting calls to true emergencies only.

Telecommuting, home office setups, cell phones and other technology allow seamless service to clients and children. Clients no longer care where their lawyer is physically located, as long as the lawyer is at the end of the phone when the client needs them. Almost anything can be done on a smart cell phone these days. Technology is advancing so quickly that staying connected is no longer a problem for anyone. Getting unplugged is a bigger issue.

One working lawyer mother told me, "I've fired clients for calling me at home on my cell phone at ten o'clock at night repeatedly, just because that's when they thought of something they wanted to tell me. If they really need me, that's one thing. But just because I gave a client my cell phone number doesn't mean they can call me whenever they feel like it." Again, it's essential to know what you can delegate, what can wait, what has to be done now, what only you can do, and what is not necessary. It's also essential to speak up for yourself in effective ways that get the point across to clients and supervising lawyers.

Multitasking is a skill most women do well. Brain science confirms that women's skills in this area exceed men's. Yet science now confirms another piece of common sense: we can only perform one task well at a time. Divided-attention tasks like driving are exceedingly difficult to perform because of the quick reaction times required. Unexpected actions of others on the road lead too quickly to disasters. Add more than one divided-attention task at a time and what you get is poor performance on all tasks. Recently science reported that teens who text message while driving are a greater danger than teens who drive under the influence of alcohol. We can't do everything at once and attempting to scatter our efforts is more harmful than helpful. The solution to this is to practice the skill of compartmentalization, which simply means to concentrate on one thing at a time. When you're at work, be fully present at work. When you're at home, be fully present at home. The work will go faster, your home life will be smoother, and the results of both will be of higher quality.

When entering a new job or returning to work after a break, all proven players must prove themselves again. In addition, all lawyers seeking career advancement must manage their professional image. This includes demonstrating they are serious about the practice; they're not just there for a paycheck, the quality of work matters to them, and client service is important to them. Mothers must also demonstrate that the work interests them enough to keep them coming in to the office; they won't bail on the client every time the baby has a cold. The fastest and most effective way to do this is to leave the family and other personal matters out of your work environment as much as possible, even in social settings. When you attend bar lunches or other quasi-social and business events, don't volunteer information about your personal life. Answer personal questions briefly and pointedly or not at all. This means no talking about the kids on the job—even at lunch with your friends—at least until you are well established. While some environments purport to be family-friendly, managing the perceptions of others requires demonstrating an understanding that work is not a paid social activity. This is a matter of managing employer expectations on the job. Leave the family talk at home and establish your professional credibility much faster. Later, if it works in your new job, you can share more personal information with coworkers.

However, reciprocity is also necessary. Successful lawyer moms leave the work life at work. When they're at home, they pay attention to family. Devoting attention to them in this way is much more effective than talking about work when your full attention should be at home with them. You'll enjoy your family time much more if you make it a point to focus on family.

Finally, lawyer moms use their lawyer personality to find time for themselves. Sleep is an absolute requirement. Studies repeatedly show that seven to seven-and-a-half hours of sleep every night is optimum for good health. Exercise is essential to keep the body strong enough for the other demands of a busy life. Eating well requires planning and some method for ensuring that healthy meals are on the table. These are non-delegable self-care duties.

Beyond the basics, moms everywhere (lawyers or not) are ingeniously carving out time for themselves. Many Web sites and magazines are devoted to these strategies and are easy to find with Google. Recently, lawyer moms have told me that they no longer clean their houses between visits from the cleaning crew; kids go with dad or grandparents on a regular weekend schedule to give mom some free time; and moms take yoga or meditation classes to reduce killer stress.

Mothers do face roadblocks that are not there for other lawyers. Fortunately, lawyer mothers are well equipped to deal with these challenges when they put their considerable mental ability to work.

PowerPlay: Stop multitasking. Devote undivided attention to one task at a time. Each task will be better and more quickly complete and you will reduce your stress levels caused by worrying about what isn't getting done.

PlugIn: Sign up for working-mom forums on the Internet and use other moms as a resource when faced with a new challenge. Ask specifically for solutions, not mere support, unless support is what you need.

Recommended Resources: *Back on the Career Track,* by Carol Fishman Cohen and Vivian Steir Rabin (Business Plus, 2007).

Best Fresh Tip: Whether you decide to reenter now or not, maintain some professional contact by volunteering on bar committees and attending professional meetings. When you're ready to reenter, you'll feel more comfortable and will have a networking base to utilize.

CHAPTER 16

Packing Your Travel Trunks

Lawyers learn to identify the goal first, and then figure out how to get there. Use that skill when deciding what you need before seeking reentry. If you were the employer you're interviewing with, why would you buy?

Realize that hiring you is a buying decision by the business. In the same way that you make a decision to buy a piece of capital equipment, a vehicle, or a house, an employer is buying you, a highly specialized bundle of human capital. The practice seeks a great investment. The partners base their hiring decision and their payment decision on that desire. But they're worried (remember, they're lawyers, too). They don't want to hire the wrong person, further drive up attrition statistics, or spend money on a mis-hire who may erode morale, client confidence, professional image, or damage firm economics. Just as you would in their shoes, they want to hire a sure thing.

Focus, then, on this question: Why are you a sure thing for this practice? What are you bringing to the table that this particular practice needs and desires? When you actually begin the interview process, you've got to believe you're doing them a favor and they're getting a great lawyer when you choose to join their practice. For lawyers, the best way to get to that mind-set is through your thinking brain.

This is a good point at which to utilize your journal and consider this question over several days. You've already been journaling regularly about what you want to do and why. It's more important to know what industry and what work you want to do than the where and how you'll do it. Now, though, it's time to turn to the where and how. Make a list of your skills. It may help you to write about past career successes and then distill your skills from those successes. What were you really good at in your last law job?

In litigation, for example, what kinds of cases did you work on and what kinds of clients did you serve? Did you try cases on your own? How many? What types? What results did you achieve? Were you successful with deposing experts? Fact witnesses? Writing briefs? Arguing motions?

For transactional lawyers, what was your most successful project? What did you do to make that project successful? During your performance reviews, what skills did your supervising lawyers identify as your strongest? If you have a copy of your last performance review, what skill categories are listed as important?

Are you good at client development? What client development experience and success have you had? For example, did you generate any new work from existing clients? What was it? Was it profitable? How did you make the work profitable?

Have you supervised staff, paralegals, or other lawyers? How many? On what types of projects? Were your supervisory skills evaluated by subordinates or superiors? What were your strengths?

Are you a strong presenter? A vivid writer? Superior extemporaneous speaker?

You're looking for your strongest skill sets in this exercise. Focusing on weaknesses is self-defeating and unimportant. Does anyone care what kind of basketball player Tiger Woods is? Does it matter that Warren Buffet may be a lousy cook or Oprah is unable to run the four-minute mile? Is it a problem that your heart surgeon sings only as well as his cat? No. What we care about, what we want from these people is for them to perform the skills they can do very, very well. The same is true of you. Your strengths are important; your weaknesses are not.

On interviews you'll be asked to identify weaknesses. I'm suggesting that you frame one of your strengths as an answer to this weakness question, too. Say your adequate delegation skills need improvement because you haven't had quality lawyers to help you in the past. Respond that you spend too much time on client development and get more work in the door than you can handle on your own. Suggest your successful skills at persuading clients to negotiate settlements need to be improved.

When you have a clear understanding of your skills, you'll be able to determine whether any need refreshing before you begin interviewing.

Rarely are rusty skill sets an impediment to reentry, but it may boost your confidence to update them.

Next, list your quantifiable successes. Some areas of accomplishment are more important to certain employers. For example, portable business is important to law firms. Particularly if you can promise new business that generates income at least twice as high as your economic cost to the firm. When an employer needs a lawyer with your specific skill set or seeks to expand into your specialized expertise, and your cost is in the right salary range, the hiring decision is easier.

Here are less obvious potential advantages you may have: you have experience in another practice doing the job they want to fill; you own a successful law practice compatible with theirs; you have a prestige background such as serving as a U.S. Supreme Court clerk; you possess a unique skill for your geographic location with potential to generate new business.

A few more obscure answers: the target employer's diversity ratio of women lawyers or minority lawyers is lower than they'd like and you're a diversity lawyer; a friend or colleague who feels secure in your suitability is now on the hiring committee; someone on the management committee is impressed with you because of recommendations from clients or colleagues.

It will not be enough for many legal employers if you have only a basic skill set or a value-added skill set in a field other than the actual practice of law, such as working in human resources, accounting, or medicine. You must be able to demonstrate a plan for adding monetary value to any private practice. For corporate legal departments and government agencies, you must add value through appropriate skills and willingness to work effectively to serve their unique clients.

Remember that you won't be hired if the practice doesn't need you. That's a given. But you won't be hired even if they do need you unless they are persuaded you suit their perceived needs. This means you should identify the needs of the practice you wish to join before you begin the interviewing process.

PowerPlay: Identify and exploit your strengths as they pertain to the job you're seeking. Ignore weaknesses. Show concrete examples to demonstrate strengths, such as number of cases tried to verdict or total dollars of revenue generated.

PlugIn: Search recruiting firm Web sites to find what employees are seeking and use that information to craft a list of your own successes.

Recommended Resource: LawJobs.com

Best Fresh Tip: Use your lawyer thinking brain to create a business case for yourself as the perfect candidate for each job you go after. Be sure to *know* you're doing them a favor, not the other way around.

CHAPTER 17

Mapping the Trip

Preparing for reentry must eventually lead to a plan for reentry and then to executing that plan. While I've learned to leave space in my plans for synchronicity, I've also learned that luck happens when preparation meets opportunity. No one is coming to rescue you. You will need to get yourself out there to find work. It's important to be visible and to let people know you want to get back in the game.

Lawyers are great planners, and we're also good at executing plans. These are skills we've developed that we often aren't aware of and don't appreciate. Your skill at planning and execution will serve you well at this stage of reentry. You've no doubt determined what kind of work you'd like to do by now, or at least narrowed your choices to fewer than five possibilities. Rank these in order of preference. Go directly for your number one choice and create a strategic plan. If you shoot for the stars and only hit the moon, you are halfway there. It's a place to start, and you can build your first-choice career from that vantage point. While you may need to reach your number one choice in stages, make as few stops as possible along the way, and every step of the process should lead toward your goal.

Years ago, when I was flying almost constantly, after multiple travel disasters I adopted a set of rules for my secretary when booking flights. One rule was never to book a flight that wasn't on a straight line to my destination. In other words, when heading from Tampa to Los Angeles, don't go by way of Chicago, even if the ticket is cheaper and regardless of the way the schedule seems to fit. The more takeoffs and landings you make along the way, the more opportunities there are for delays, lost luggage, missed connections, and so forth. These are good rules for goal achievement, too.

Perhaps you've decided to leave law practice entirely and work in another arena. A law degree is a flexible asset that many use to launch nonlegal careers in finance, consulting, human resources, sales, education, politics, and many other fields. If your work experience is entirely law related, reentry into a different field will present additional challenges. You'll be starting at the bottom of the experience ladder and the bottom of the pay scale. You'll also be expected to pay your dues like anyone else starting out in that field. If the work energizes you enough to help you slug through these challenges, fine. If not, be aware that you're adding to your load by making a total career change.

Another possibility many lawyers consider on reentry is starting a nonlegal business or franchise. Certainly many lawyers are astute business people. Joint J.D. and M.B.A. programs are common in many universities, so you may have a business background as well. Start-up businesses require an entrepreneurial personality and mind-set. They also require a valid funding strategy. Being a business owner can be even more time-and-energy-consuming than the full-time practice of law. But owning one's business is an exciting goal that can provide significant personal and financial reward.

Starting or joining a legal-related business, such as recruiting, training, consulting, sales for legal products, or temporary legal services, is another possibility for reentry. Being a lawyer enhances your resumé for these jobs. You will be working with lawyers but not practicing law. In corporate law departments or government agencies, these roles are typically filled in-house or by vendors approved through corporate or agency processes, which can be daunting. In these businesses, law firms of various sizes and individual lawyers are the main source of customers, which presents challenges for many businesses. Lawyers and law practices present a longer than normal buying cycle. The lawyer personality leads to roadblocks that don't occur as frequently with non-lawyer customers. These challenges are not insurmountable, but strategic planning is required to conquer them and succeed in building and growing a business.

Most reentry lawyers settle on either a traditional full-time position as a practicing lawyer, working as a part-time lawyer, doing freelance contract legal work, or starting their own law firm. Speaking from personal experience, each of these options presents challenges and rewards. In many ways, every lawyer is a solo practitioner regardless of the forum in which she or he practices. As professionals, we come together in groups, but client responsibility is often ours alone. We work in teams that include support staff, so we have leadership and human resources responsibilities. As our practices grow, we hire, train, and supervise junior lawyers. We set fee arrangements with clients and must deal with collections, so we have financial responsibilities. Our compensation is often dependent first on profits of the enterprise and then our contributions.

Starting your own law firm is always an option for lawyers and one many lawyers love. If you have practiced in a law firm before and had some exposure or experience with law practice management, you stand a better chance of success at owning and operating your own firm. You need start-up capital and clients or the ability to acquire clients to begin. After that, you can build your practice into one that suits your personal needs.

Regardless of which reentry position you decide to pursue, you will need a plan and a few tools to get there. Spend some time creating your resumé and make it as good as possible. There are many resources available to help you with this project if you need assistance. I suggest creating a longer, comprehensive resumé that can be customized to particular opportunities as well as a one-page and a two-page resumé. Be absolutely certain that your resumé does not contain any errors before you submit it anywhere. When you begin your job search, you will often need your resumé on a moment's notice, so always keep current copies available in hard copy and a file on your home computer. Update your resumé regularly, at least every six months. Don't list references on your resumé. Create a separate list of references that can be submitted on short notice.

Even in our electronic age, don't post your resumé to job boards or Web sites. And consider using a post office box if you must list your address. Don't give prospective employers or clients your home telephone number; give them a cell number instead and never allow anyone to answer your cell except you.

You will need to be prepared to explain your resumé gaps. Plan your responses in advance and use your precise visualization techniques to get comfortable with delivering your explanation. Be honest and straightforward about your career break, but frame it as positively as possible. For example, if you took a career break to rear children, say that, but add that you're now eager to return to work because you've missed the practice, or you miss working with clients, or give another business reason for returning to work. You'll receive conflicting advice on this, but I believe, if asked, you should admit that you need the money if that's true. Legal employers want to know that you're highly motivated to work and some appreciate your being hungry. Once again, frame this in a way that makes you more desirable as a candidate. Above all, you must persuade potential employers that you are committed to the job. This is the underlying fear that keeps them from taking a chance on you. They worry you'll bail when they need you the most. They must know they can count on you when they need you there.

In addition to a well-selected reentry position, a strong resumé, a great writing sample, and a well-delivered explanation for both your break in service and your reason for returning at this time to this employer, you will need time and a good network. Finding the right opportunity will take awhile. The longer your time horizon, the less stress you'll experience during the process. There will inevitably be rejections, bad interviews, and opportunities lost along the way. It's easier to take these in stride and learn from them if you have the luxury of time on your side. If you do need to make money right away, as mentioned earlier, the fastest way to generate cash as a lawyer is through temporary agencies and contract work. These are also good part-time jobs for lawyers, although they may not pay as well as you need.

Your network is your million-dollar Rolodex. As I mentioned earlier, more jobs are found through personal contacts than any other means. Your network is also the foundation of your life in business and in every other aspect. It exists for one reason only: to build relationships so we can help each other. Everyone gets by with a little help from our friends, not just John, Paul, George, and Ringo. It consists of everyone you've ever known, the people in your life now, and people you will meet in the future. These days it includes your Facebook friends and your Twitter followers too. If you don't have a computerized mailing list, now is the time to create one and maintain it for the rest of your life. Put it in an Excel spreadsheet where it can be imported into many other programs. Add to it as you meet new people. This list will be the starting point for everyone you need in life. The full scope of effective networking is beyond the limitations of this book, but there are many resources available to you. Again, a quick Google search will bring up an overwhelming number of options. The basic point for now is that you should be looking to find people who can help you get the job you want, and you must be ready, willing, and able to help them get something they want first.

These are the basics of a great reentry plan. Your plan will be specific to your personal needs and desires. It should be strategic, not just a form from a book. The goal is to get the job you want at this point in your life. As you are unique, the plan must be unique, too.

PowerPlay: Consider alternative careers as well as alternative employers and work schedules. If you rule out undesirable alternatives, you can more easily narrow your focus. When you decide on your number one choice, go for it directly, head on, not with an oblique approach.

PlugIn: Use your network to find an entrée to the positions you identify as your number one goal.

Recommended Resource: *The Creative Lawyer: A Practical Guide to Authentic Professional Satisfaction*, by Michael F. Melcher (American Bar Association, 2007); *This Year I Will*, by M. J. Ryan (Broadway Books, 2006); *201 Best Questions to Ask on Your Interview*, by John Kador (McGraw-Hill, 2002); *Over-40 Job Search Guide*, by Gail Geary (JIST Works, 2005).

Best Fresh Tip: Use the three-phone-call rule which posits that, at certain levels of American life, everyone can be connected in three phone calls. When you identify your number one employment target, use your network to find the best way to approach the position and the best person to help you.

CHAPTER 18

Women Drivers

Women-owned businesses have been the fastest-growing segment of the U.S. economy for more than ten years. At this writing, women own 41 percent of all privately held companies, according to the Center for Business Research. Those businesses employ 13 million people and spend $546 billion each year on salaries and benefits. In 2008, women-owned businesses poured $1.9 trillion into the national economy.

A recent study by the Caliper Corporation of 59 women business leaders in 19 different business sectors in the U.S. and the U.K. reveals a few surprises. Caliper found women leaders differ from men in four significant respects. Women are more assertive and persuasive; are more likely to ignore rules and take risks; have an inclusive, team-building style of leadership and problem solving; and "feel the sting of rejection, learn from adversity, and carry on with an 'I'll show you' attitude." (From "The Qualities That Distinguish Women Leaders," an article published online at http://www.caliperonline.com/womenstudy/WomenLeader-WhitePaper.pdf.)

These leadership qualities are apparent in women lawyers, making them valuable assets to firms and business. Such traits may also be why women have been leaving the legal profession in disproportionately high numbers for more than ten years and why they don't go back. Research published in 2004 by Catalyst, a group whose mission is to advance and expand the role of women in business, found that women feel pushed out of law firms by inequitable treatment rather than pulled out by family or other demands. It also established that companies with the highest representation of women in top management outperform their competitors financially. (For the full research report, see http://www.catalyst.org/publication/82/the-bottom-line-connecting-corporate-performance-and-gender-diversity.) Results reported by Harvard Business

Review were similarly impressive: companies with high numbers of women executives posted profits that were from 18 to 69 percent better than companies with fewer women executives. (See Sylvia Ann Hewlett's *Off-Ramps and On-Ramps*, page 104.)

The American Bar Association's Commission on Women in the Profession study entitled "Visible Invisibility" found that women of color were even more likely to leave because they felt other opportunities were more lucrative, decisions about their careers would be based on merit, and other jobs would allow better work-life balance. (See http://www.abanet.org/women/VisibleInvisibility-ExecSummary.pdf.)

The Project for Attorney Retention (http://www.pardc.org) reports that law firms are behind the curve in providing balanced-hours policies when compared to other businesses and suggests methods for improving retention through balanced-hour plans.

Women desiring to reenter the workforce should read these studies and make a career plan accordingly. At a minimum, these organizations provide information that can be used to maximize a reentry to traditional law firm practice. By using the data contained in the studies, a strong business case can be made for adding qualified women to the payroll of any organization.

PowerPlay: Consider launching your own firm, either practicing law or another business. When you are the business owner, you have maximum flexibility and control—which means you must learn how to use both to your personal and professional satisfaction.

PlugIn: Prepare a business case for your desired employment plan. Practice the case with knowledgeable mentors or colleagues to improve and perfect the presentation. Present the case when you interview for desired positions.

Recommended Resources: Web sites such as those referenced above provide the most current information; subscribe to http://connectwellconsulting.com, where we deal regularly with law practice issues specifically responsive to your individual concerns.

Best Fresh Tip: Consider attending programs such as Harvard Business School's "A New Path," launched in 2006, a weeklong program to prepare women to reenter the workforce.

CONCLUSION

Practicing law is one of the most flexible, lucrative, fulfilling, intellectually stimulating, and rewarding professions available to Americans today. The lawyer personality drives our desire for success, for excellent performance, and for client service. While these challenges can be overwhelming, lawyers are uniquely competent to manage their lives and their work effectively.

Legal careers can and often do span more than fifty years. As long as lawyers remain healthy and engaged with the practice, they can be productive members of the bar and society for the entire length of their lives. Taking a break from law practice is normal, worthwhile, and manageable. Returning to practice afterward is not an insurmountable brick wall, but an opportunity to strategically build and improve upon the last level of practice achieved.

"Life is either a daring adventure or nothing," Helen Keller famously told us. The same can be true of the practice of law. Truly, it's up to you.

APPENDIX A

PowerPlays

- Realize that taking a career break isn't the end of your legal career. Talk to other lawyers and you'll find many who've done exactly what you're seeking to do now.
- Ask better questions as you plan your reentry strategy. In a world where anything can be done, what's worth doing? What is strategically (not just logically) next? Who can help you? What is the easiest way to get to the next destination?
- Begin to consider developing your lifelong Platinum Practice™ as you contemplate reentry, using more optimism and less pessimism.
- Determine which phase of the reentry process you're resting in now and whether you're ready to move to the next phase. If you're not ready now, when will you be ready?
- Get your head in the game by using your thinking brain to craft an optimistic plan exciting to your emotional brain. Use precise visualization to experience and refine the plan as well as reduce any potential stress associated with implementing the plan.
- Get inspired. Find extraordinary women lawyers to consider as professional role models, whether you meet them or not. Most have had similar work experiences and have spent time out of the active workforce.
- Recognize and acknowledge your goal as an achievable activity. Work is an essential element of human happiness and a strong element of life balance. Balance is something you do, not something you have; constant effort is required to obtain and maintain balance.
- Experts agree that the ideal solution is to develop a long-term relationship with one employer, investing at least five years of employment up front before your break and negotiating your return before you leave.
- Recognize this journey is an opportunity to improve your life, not a chore. Use the power of precise visualization to secure an Olympic gold medal in job satisfaction. See your new job as a done deal and feel its impact on your life. Lest this seem a bit too new age for lawyers, realize that you need to know what you're seeking before you can recognize it, know where to look for it or grab it when you find it.

- Become a best lawyer to obtain the highest possible levels of job satisfaction and the most appropriate compensation. Go after the best lawyer characteristics directly.
- Begin creating a great plan for reentry designed to go directly for the job you want. The plan may require initial employment in a short-term job to gain experience in a particular field or additional training before moving up to the job you're seeking.
- Large law firms present challenges for reentering lawyers, but also significant potential. Find as many connections between you and the firm as possible. Create a strategic plan for approaching and joining the firm.
- Be self-sufficient when it comes to office technology to broaden your appeal to law practices of all sizes and increase the job's flexibility to suit your needs. Understand how computers store data to avoid inadvertent disclosure of client-sensitive information.
- Don't be dysfunctionally independent. Delegate everything you can delegate and only do what's truly necessary yourself. Err on the side of delegating to allow more time for self-care if family members are well cared for by others.
- Stop multitasking. Devote undivided attention to one task at a time. Each task will be better and more quickly complete and you will reduce your stress levels caused by worrying about what isn't getting done.
- Identify and exploit your strengths as they pertain to the job you're seeking. Ignore weaknesses. Show concrete examples to demonstrate strengths, such as number of cases tried to verdict or total dollars of revenue generated.
- Consider alternative careers as well as alternative employers and work schedules. If you rule out undesirable alternatives, you can more easily narrow your focus. When you decide on your number one choice, go for it directly, head on, not in an oblique approach.
- Consider launching your own firm, either practicing law or another business. When you are the business owner, you have maximum flexibility and control—which means you must learn how to use both to your personal and professional satisfaction.

APPENDIX B

PlugIns

- Get clear on your motivation. Why haven't you returned to work? Why do you want to do it now?
- Join the Platinum Practice™ community at http://www.connectwellconsulting.com for innovative strategic solutions, information, and tips that work.
- Knowing lawyers are skeptical by nature suggests you may be looking for proof of this information right now. For a revealing explanation of common traits of the lawyer personality, see "Herding Cats: The Lawyer Personality Revealed," an article by Larry R. Richard (Hildebrandt International Publications/Press Room, 2009), at http://hildebrandt.com/Documents.aspx?Doc_ID=2430.
- Give yourself some deadlines for moving through each of the phases of reentry. The length of time you spend in each phase is less important than moving forward. Will you remain where you are for another hour? Another year? Creating a deadline will keep the goal on your mental radar and help you make progress.
- Avoid commiserating with or wallowing in any form of negativity while you're planning and seeking reentry, because precise visualization works to create negative as well as positive results. Keep a positive mental attitude and remember Justices O'Connor and Ginsberg when your lawyer's pessimism threatens.
- Find a local woman lawyer who has achieved the reentry you hope to accomplish. Schedule a meeting with her and ask her how she managed to do what you seek to do. If you can't find one, contact me, and I'll help you look. Contact me at diane@connectwellconsulting.com.
- Create a great plan with a strategic execution timeline. Reentry, defined as any major transition from one type of employment or unemployment to reemployment, is inevitable and inevitably successful.
- Stay connected to your employer, colleagues, and other alumni groups. If you've allowed too much time between contacts, resume now.
- Use a journal to tap into your subconscious for answers. Writing your way from here to there is one of the most reliable methods for uncovering a successful reentry target. Little things mean a great

deal more than you might at first believe. Annoyances add up and can become too burdensome. Try on your new job and see if you like it before you expend any shoe leather. What do you feel when you think of your new job? What do you look like while you're doing it? What do the offices smell like? What's the view outside your window? Who are your clients? Why do they need you? Why are you the perfect lawyer for them? Why is this job perfect for you now?

- Make peace with money as an exchange of energy for dollars. What do you bring to the table? Be sure you get adequately compensated for your contribution. Identify your value to yourself, your family, and your work in dollars and cents to determine whether you need a paying job or not and to set appropriate salary goals for reentry.
- Be strategic in your reentry plan to avoid choice fatigue and paralysis by analysis caused by the overwhelming number of options available to today's job seekers. Don't get swamped by dismal statistics and horror stories. Stay focused on creating and working your plan.
- Ignore the negative and stay focused on the positive aspects of large firm practice. Take personal responsibility for creating a successful career within the realities.
- Buy a smart phone and learn to use it. Use your home computer to your best advantage by learning necessary computer skills before you return to work. Take at least one online CLE course on the new Federal Rules of Civil Procedure governing the handling of electronic data to avoid unwittingly jeopardizing your client's confidential communications and your work-product privilege.
- Keep your own calendar. Do not allow anyone to schedule anything on your calendar without your express consent.
- Sign up for working-mom forums on the Internet and use other moms as a resource when faced with a new challenge. Ask specifically for solutions, not mere support, unless support is what you need.
- Search recruiting firm Web sites to find what employees are seeking and use that information to craft a list of your own successes.
- Use your network to find an entrée to the positions you identify as your number one goal.
- Prepare a business case for your desired employment plan. Practice the case with knowledgeable mentors or colleagues to improve and perfect the presentation. Present the case when you interview for desired positions.

APPENDIX C

Recommended Reading

Authentic Happiness, by Martin E. P. Seligman (Free Press, 2004).

Back on the Career Track, by Carol Fishman Cohen and Vivian Steir Rabin (Business Plus, 2007).

The Comeback: Seven Stories of Women Who Went from Career to Family and Back Again, by Emma Gilbey Keller, 2008 (Bloomsbury USA, 2008).

The Complete Guide to Contract Lawyering: What Every Lawyer and Law Firm Needs to Know About Temporary Legal Service, by Deborah Arron and Deborah Guyol (Niche Press, 1999).

ConnectWell Consulting's *Journal Your Way There* classes.

The Creative Lawyer: A Practical Guide to Authentic Professional Satisfaction, by Michael F. Melcher (American Bar Association, 2007).

Getting A Life, by Jacqueline Blix and David Heitmiller (Viking, 1997).

Happiness: Unlocking the Mysteries of Psychological Wealth, by Ed Diener and Robert Biswas-Diener (Wiley-Blackwell, 2008).

How to Start and Build a Law Practice, by Jay Foonberg (American Bar Association, 2004).

Keeping Good Lawyers: Best Practices to Create Career Satisfaction, by M. Diane Vogt and Lori-Ann Rickard (Law Practice Management Section, American Bar Association, 2000).

Keeping a Journal You Love, by Sheila Bender (Walking Stick Press, 2001).

Off-Ramps and On-Ramps: Keeping Talented Women on the Road to Success, by Sylvia Ann Hewlett (Harvard Business School Press, 2007).

Over-40 Job Search Guide, by Gail Geary (JIST Works, 2005).

Psychological Foundations of Success: A Harvard-Trained Scientist Separates the Science of Success from Self-Help Snake Oil, by Stephen Kraus (Next Level Science, 2003).

Sandra Day O'Connor: Justice in the Balance, by Ann Carey McFeatters (University of New Mexico Press, 2006).

Secrets of Six-Figure Women, by Barbara Stanny (Harper Business, 2004).

Technology in the Law Office, byThomas F. Goldman (Prentice Hall, 2007).

This Year I Will, by M. J. Ryan (Broadway Books, 2006)

201 Best Questions to Ask on Your Interview, by John Kador (McGraw-Hill, 2002)

What Color Is Your Parachute, by Richard Nelson Bolles (Ten Speed Press).

Your Money or Your Life: 9 Steps to Transforming Your Relationship with Money and Achieving Financial Independence:Revised and Updated for the 21st Century, by Joe Dominguez and Vicki Robin (Penguin, 2008).

Web sites

http://backonthecareertrack.com/
http://connectwellconsulting.com
LawJobs.com
Project for Attorney Retention, at http://www.pardc.org/

APPENDIX D

Best Fresh Tip

- Do you have grit? People with grit are more likely to achieve, maybe because their passion and commitment help them endure through setbacks. Develop grit by making a commitment and sticking with it.
- Take the joy road, the easy way, to creating your Platinum Practice™.
- Recognize the common aspects of the lawyer personality and use them effectively when creating your Platinum Practice™.
- Consider framing your goals as pleasure seeking rather than pain avoidance, to increase desire and enthusiasm and prepare for achievement. How does the more positive frame make you feel?Can your emotional brain get behind the pleasure-seeking process? Can your thinking brain get out of the way?
- Get reconnected to your local bar associations. Attend meetings and mingle with other lawyers. Ask lawyers if they've ever taken a break from the practice of law and, if so, how they managed reentry. The number of success stories you hear will boost your visualization and spirits.
- Allow inspiration to lead you forward toward your own goals, whether your goals are the same as the achievements of others or not.
- Unsure of what new jobs to consider? Check out the Caliper Profile (http://caliperonline.com/), a personality profiling method used to profile more than 1,000 lawyers. Harold Weinstein, chief operating officer of Caliper Corporation, noted that "People who are working in roles that are consistent with their personality, values and interpersonal characteristics generally outperform those who are less well matched—by a ratio of two-to-one."
- Develop the skills necessary to find appropriate mentors for your current situation. Mentors are more important to your long-term career success than any other single factor.
- Make job satisfaction your first goal. This means going after personal happiness first, not expecting happiness to come to you as a reward for selfless service and sacrifice. Well-satisfied lawyers report their priorities in this order:
  - Self, family, colleagues, and mentors
  - Workplace flexibility

- Personal control over most aspects of the job
- Freedom to design a satisfying career
- Compensation

- Corporations don't often hire entry-level lawyers, which means you'll have an experience advantage if you choose to apply. Be realistic about your compensation prospects, neither over- nor underestimating your value. Accurate data about compensation is difficult to find because compensation ranges for lawyers vary widely due to subjective and objective factors. Recruiters often possess salary information they are willing to share without identifying the specific private employer. Government agency, law school, and corporation salaries for lawyers can be obtained online. Check, e.g., information.com for law firm salaries; and *Law Department Compensation Benchmarking Survey*, published annually by Altman Weil, Inc., at http://www.altmanweil.com. For government agency salaries, you can contact the agency directly or the relevant bar association.
- A few universities, businesses, and bar associations offer seminars and classes to assist you with preparations to reenter the workforce. Use these if you feel the need, but make the most of the opportunity by networking effectively before, during, and after the seminars.
- Consider alumni associations (law school, college, high school, past employers); better yet, start an alumni association using the Internet. Contact connectwell.com for our white paper on creating a powerful alumni group.
- Use bar review courses to update your substantive legal skills or learn new areas of the law quickly and accurately.
- If you want to work balanced hours in your current practice, the key issue is whether supervising attorneys are on board. Help them get there by making a business case for your plan.
- Whether you decide to reenter now or not, maintain some professional contact by volunteering on bar committees and attending professional meetings. When you're ready to reenter, you'll feel more comfortable and will have a networking base to utilize.
- Use your lawyer thinking brain to create a business case for yourself as the perfect candidate for each job you go after. Be sure to *know* you're doing them a favor, not the other way around.
- Use the three-phone-call rule which posits that, at certain levels of American life, everyone can be connected in three phone calls. When you identify your number one employment target, use your

network to find the best way to approach the position and the best person to help you.

- Consider attending programs such as Harvard Business School's "A New Path," launched in 2006, a weeklong program to prepare women to reenter the workforce.

INDEX

ABOUT THE AUTHOR

M. Diane Vogt, Esq., is the Managing Member of ConnectWell Consulting LLC (http://www.connectwellconsulting.com) and a practicing lawyer for more than twenty-eight years.

ConnectWell Consulting LLC's mission is to keep good lawyers well connected to extraordinary careers, whether those careers take traditional, non-traditional, linear, or non-linear paths.

ConnectWell Consulting LLC works directly with individual lawyers as well as law firms, agencies, and law departments. ConnectWell Consulting LLC's website contains information on available services and classes.

Diane is the author of seven books, short stories, and numerous articles on a variety of subjects. She's been interviewed on television and radio stations around the country. Diane has presented materials on law practice management and keeping good lawyers engaged in the practice to the Annual Meetings of the American Bar Association, State Bar of Michigan, Florida Bar Association, National Association of Law Placement, Association of Legal Administrators, Defense Research Institute, and many more. In addition, she has presented to state and local bar associations around the country on issues related to law practice and job satisfaction for lawyers.

A 1980 cum laude graduate of Wayne Law School where she was a junior and senior member of the Law Review, Diane was admitted to the Michigan Bar in 1980 and the Florida Bar in 1989, where she continues to practice. She has been "AV" rated by Martindale-Hubbell Law Directory in both Detroit and Tampa since 1990 and 1994, respectively. She was named a member of the inaugural Florida Legal Elite, and selected for inclusion in various meritorious and honorary societies.